"This is a deeply honest and touching story of a father's deep love for his family. It is a reminder that even though we devote so much of ourselves into envisioning and planning our dreams, we cannot always protect ourselves and those we love from devastating tragedy. This poetic prose relays how a family can be shattered by the violence of drunk driving which killed his son, Adam. John gripped my heart as he took me on a journey of passionate family devotion."

—*Jan Withers, National President*
Mothers Against Drunk Driving

Sarah & Ray

Only godness &
love

JD

Return to the Water

a father's account of reconciling his
own past and keeping a family together
after losing a son

Return to the Water

a father's account of reconciling his
own past and keeping a family together
after losing a son

JOHN STEPHENS

LIBRARY OF CONGRESS CATALOGUING
IN PUBLICATION DATA
Stephens, John
Memoir. Prose.
ISBN 13: 978-1-936196-29-6

C&R Press
812 Westwood Ave.
Suite D
Chattanooga, TN 37405
www.crpress.org

Book Design: HSDesigns
Cover art: HSDesigns

Edited by Katie Chaple & Travis Denton

In partnership with Eco-Libris, 100 trees
have been planted toward the creation of
this book. For more about Eco-Libris and
making reading more sustainable, please
visit www.ecolibris.net.

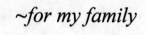

~for my family

Acknowledgements:

Thanks to Anna, Adam, Hanna, Olivia and Sofia for all their wonders. Thanks to Tom and Jenny Lux for their love and friendship; to Travis Denton and Kate Chaple for their support, love and the good things they gave us as we took a journey together; to my friends, Jedwin, Dave, Julie, Boyd, Chad, Barry and Mr. Weinstein's Atlanta Writers Club members who listened to me read from this work over all those years; to my sister Lynn and her two Rogers who took the right course; to the Moran family who gives so much to so many with such grace; to Karen's poetry group, and many others. And a special thanks to Poetry@Tech for their support in establishing the Adam Stephens Night Out for Poetry, so he is always remembered.

table of contents

Prologue

chapter

Prologue

Fatherhood was never meant to be like this.

Today, your mother should be anticipating another Mother's Day gift, the Good & Plenty candies you always left on her pillow. Your three sisters should be looking forward to each day, knowing their big brother would be there to help them through troubles with boys, love, or to just know you're around. I should be laughing at the thought of your first beer when we talked about music, tennis, and your adolescent philosophies, you telling me stories that were so full of magic and plans.

Right now, I am looking at the clock, knowing the anniversary hour approaches. But not an anniversary that anyone wants. Instead, I hear the whispers of another stack of hours between night and morning—all possessed by anger, because I know that we no longer can hold you. It has been an agonizing year; there are these images that are burned as a shroud in my skull, which can never be. Adam.

There are those who tell me I think too much, that I dwell too much on the past. Instead of holding you close to my heart, Adam, they tell me I should "move on," such a callous phrase. To forget you seems sacrilege. It is an act I am incapable of.

As I write this, it's as if I'm living what I know of your life in reverse. I'm reliving each detail of your final hours—your last days of high school, your afternoons spent with your sisters and mother and the ones you loved most preparing for your graduation.

Son, you told your mother before you walked out of the house, "I love you, Mom." You laughed. "Don't worry, everything will be all right." She went to bed. And then you stepped into the night.

The doorbell rang too early that morning. Anna hesitantly opened the front door to two officers standing there, ill-at-ease. They said, "Your son has been in an accident."

"Where is he?" she asked.

"He did not make it."

And so your mother's screams woke your sisters, who raced down the stairs to confront grief, to join her in her sobbing.

I was not home. I was 2,500 miles and three hours time difference away. I was lying awake reading and would learn about you in a phone call—my wife, your mother, panicked and screaming.

You were taken from us by the selfish, irresponsible act of your drunken buddy. He had the gall to approach me three days later at your funeral and say, "Adam came to me last night and told me, 'It's okay, Andrew.'" It was as if he was still drunk to think he could even speak your name to me.

It's not okay, Son. Maybe that statement made Andrew feel better, but I know it doesn't work that way. If there is, indeed, a direct line between heaven and those of us on Earth, I'm sure you would have assured your mother or your sisters, or even me—not the person responsible for your death.

Anger and depression are part of a brutal process, Son. It's going to take an awful lot of time for me, for all of us, to work through this. That's why I put everything down on paper for your mom and your sisters. I should have shared everything with you earlier, Adam, so you could have all those opportunities to see how much we love you.

Call this a living testimonial, if you will. I go back and forth in my mind, recalling each detail of our time. Your pictures are everywhere in our bedroom, your urn sits nearby. I often go to your bedroom to touch the tennis rackets, look down the microscope, wondering what you saw under its light. I put on your sunglasses, sit in your chair, running my fingers over your computer keys. I open the desk drawers to read your notes, hold those items that you kept so close to you. I read then re-read one note you left yourself titled "4 me." It starts with, "Be more happy, make Stephanie fall more in love with me, find more hobbies to do, learn programming, don't talk back to people." I fold it, carefully putting it back in its place, knowing you would have done them all.

Today is dark. That's what happens when life is snatched away.

Even though I'm blessed by the unconditional love of your mother and sisters, I feel alone now. I recite The Lord's Prayer constantly. We are told angels are never far, but my loss has numbed that thought. Even now, as the anniversary hour approaches, my tears flow as I dial your cell phone number yet again, just to hear your voice on the recording.

Until we meet again, I clutch at memories.

1 To Begin

Certain impressions are often unforgettable: your first love, the birth of a child, the first meeting of those who will become lifelong friends, or even the opening pages of a new book. Everything has its inception.

For me, it started on the shores of Lake Hjälmaren in Lappe, Sweden, an uncomplicated place, where I began reading Hemingway's *The Sun Also Rises*.

Sweden's summer sun never really sets. Its orange, faded glow is everywhere all the time. Throughout the course of the day, dark clouds and rain showers try, yet fail, to mar that country's glow. The Northern skies are always abundant and though littered with clouds, they are radiant.

The day I began reading Hemingway's book, the sky was clear, the air clean as crisp wind, no cloud to shade the sunlight.

Our family's small lodging was a couple hundred feet from the lake's rocky shoreline. Occasional rain drops and ripples pushed against the shore, and each day brought a Scandinavian calmness. As I peered across the lake, I could barely rise from the chair. Laziness consumed me. Nature was in its zenith; the scenery contrasted with the wrenching of modern civilization.

I moved slowly, taking care of basic wants, having coffee, mingling with close friends and family, while contemplating the day's needs, possibly a meal.

Over the years Anna and I have often traveled to Lake Hjälmaren—her summer home. It was here, in her youth, that Anna spent her vacations with her brother and two sisters, where her mother, Siv, grew up with her family as a little girl.

On our first trip as a new family, we brought our firstborn, Adam. Anna and I had spoken about this lake many times and decided Lake Hjälmaren—this fresh, clean body of water, this conduit of family—would be the perfect place for our children to be baptized. Adam was less than a year old when he first came to Sweden. All of Anna's family traveled to this sun-drenched spot. We prepared an abundance of food, fish, cheese, breads and cakes the night before. The ladies unpacked, cleaned and put on their traditional Swedish folk dresses which were worn by three generations of the family's women. The pastor came early, knew all the family members but me, and on the lawn, in his white robe, he began a ceremony that had been recounted time and again at this same place, under these very trees. On that day, with all the family gathered, Adam was baptized. The scripture, though read in Swedish, was like a song to me.

Although I didn't understand God's words in Anna's language, all that mattered was the magnitude of the event. No translation was necessary—the beauty of the words, the rise and fall of each syllable, each sound was enough.

As the weeks passed and I continued my reading, I didn't need a bookmark. I could remember exactly where I left off, always at the top of a page.

I didn't stop with Hemingway's stories of manhood. That trip with Adam's baptism, my initiation, marked the beginning of my own journey as a reader and a writer. I continued to read one classic after another—*East of Eden*, where you feel their pains, and even their simple pleasures in some lantern lit room—*The Sound and the Fury*, where brothers' plots are as difficult to follow as their three voices sweep within the second hands of the clocks, *The Brothers Karamazov* whose ending cry, "Hurrah for Karamazov" stuns you, as you scream it out. I found time daily to turn the page, whether it was on an airplane or in the middle of the night, having been jarred awake by some sound or thought. I consumed books in this fashion for more than eighteen years. Each page replacing the day's nagging worries. I soon wondered if I could put words together, like an author. It seemed a noble thing to do. I bought a red notebook and wrote the first page of this new beginning. I took the journal with us, kept filling it with words, compiling it page by page, place by place. I purposefully left the journal around the house so Anna, Adam, Hanna, Olivia, and Sofia could read it. But I mostly read it to them; they supplied the corrections. I was glad for that, since I wrote about them; they were my heroes and heroines, and I needed to get the details just right, since the stories were to be everyone's memories.

The stories were about family—simple observations about places we traveled together, our good times, and my nightmares.

It was my intention to publish five first-editions of this journal, which were to be given to each of them upon my death. A hand-written note would accompany each book on the inside cover, signed: "Love, Papa."

Of course, they were well aware I was compiling the journal. One or two would gather on a bed as I read the stories aloud—their stories—and without fail they would add their own observations.

Not everything I wrote was upbeat. I wrote about my youth, about my tribulations growing up, the kind I did not want for them.

I was twelve when my parents divorced. Until that jarring event, each of my weekdays had been the same: I walked to the bus stop in the mornings, and walked home in the afternoons—what happened between was just a typical school day. I could see our house when I turned down the street, one house from the corner.

One day in sixth grade, I walked home to see a sheriff's car and a white van parked in our driveway. My mother was waiting for me as I ran up the drive, cigarette burning between her fingers. A locksmith stood next to her at work on the front door.

Looking at me, Mom tossed the cigarette to the ground,

"We're going on vacation. Can you get the luggage down from the attic?"

Normally I liked going into the attic. It was a place of solitude. But that day it felt cold, just dark—a hiding place.

"Hurry up," my mother kept yelling.

In my haste, I dropped the brown, hard-shelled suitcases down the ladder, with her answering scream, "What the hell was that?"

I grabbed the suitcases and apologized. And that's when she said "We're going alone. Your father's not coming."

There had been problems between them for some time. They couldn't keep that a secret—never tried. She didn't admit it, but I knew she was running that day. She had the processor throw Dad out when he got home from work; she liked to get others to do her dirty work.

My younger brother James and sister Lynn sat quietly while Mom packed the suitcases. Then a process server—a large man with dark eyes, a jutting jaw, and a grim stare— walked in the front door. His commanding profile and swift glance toward us showed no signs of compassion.

The locksmith handed the new keys to my mother and to the processor.

"Get in the car," Mom commanded.

I sat with my siblings in the green station wagon, while my mother talked with the men. I was detached, and I wondered what my father would do when he got home. I wondered what the processor would say to him. Most of all, I wondered how we would manage without him.

When Mom jumped into the car and turned the key, the engine startled me out of my daydream.

"It'll be alright," Mom told us as we drove off. Her hand trembled as she pushed in the cigarette lighter. That afternoon we ended up at a hotel along the freeway, not far from home. We stayed here for a night or two. I guess what she did was protocol: locks that don't work with the keys he left with in the morning, a lifeless house, so fathers get the message that they're no longer wanted. Mom left us first at the hotel pool, then the restaurant, when a man we'd never seen before, her lawyer, arrived with documents for her to sign.

My father tried to reconcile at first, but it was a violent marriage that turned into a bitter divorce. My mother did all she could to brainwash us; we had the propaganda down pat, telling the judge what an awful person our father was, how he beat our mother, abused her. I'm sure what we said must have hurt him. Once the divorce was finalized, Mom got the house, money, and three kids. Our family life ended just like that.

Mom told us she would have to get a job to support our lifestyle, but it was a means for her to meet other men, to play bridge, and to drink, all under the economic illusion she created in her mind, just for us.

Dad stayed around for a year or two, then without warning moved to San Francisco, leaving us behind for a new job. He was that kind of man—understandably hurt, but selfish. He went through two more marriages, and so did my mother.

As for us kids? We were just along for the ride.

I ended up leaving home right out of high school, living in a two-bedroom apartment with my brother and an older boy, Kurt Venzor. Dad did support us, but he held his money over our heads, manipulating us with demands to go do this or that in exchange for some monetary support or the like—promises that he never really intended to keep. His concept of parental care was an equal mix of lies and self-centeredness. My brother lasted only two months on his own in that apartment before moving back home to live with our mother and sister.

My mother's drink of choice was and is vodka and orange juice, and I can't remember any length of time when she remained sober. She had a tight bond with James, who at a young age qualified for gifted education; this set him apart from the rest of us in her mind. She knew that it was from her that he got his gifts. She loved to listen to him play his guitar. They fed off each other's attention.

My baby sister Lynn was about five when my parents split.

Then, at the tender age of ten, she was on the receiving end of the worst of our mother's abuse. I stopped by the house one day to discover that Lynn had locked herself in her room, the window wide open, letting in fresh air, or maybe to escape through. Mom was passed out on the couch, her drinks littering the glass table—some empty, some half-full, and always one with ice melting. The stench of alcohol and dog-shit was overpowering. The house was filthy, beyond disgusting. I telephoned my father, telling him about his daughter's living conditions, and he finally came one evening and took Lynn with him.

I neither admired nor trusted my parents.

For as long as I can remember, I wanted a loving father and mother, a family that took vacations, a safe place to go home to, but that would not happen with these two.

2 My Family

Scott Munro, a friend of mine since childhood, telephoned and said he knew four Swedish girls who were looking to go out for a night on the town and was I interested?

I was twenty-eight, living like I was eighteen, looking for someone every night, drinking too much, living the California life where cars and money defined you. It was a façade I didn't want and was no good at. I needed something meaningful, someone to make a life with. The first time I met Anna, it was obvious she was very different than the local girls. Her Swedish accent, her desire to experience the unexpected, her aloof attitude captivated me the moment I met her.

Scott is what I'd call an eternal optimist. He borders on being overzealous. So I really didn't know what to expect of the girls or the evening. But once he described the young ladies and their enthusiasm, I was convinced. I wanted everything he said to be true, but then again, what did I care—it sounded like good times were to be had and not truly knowing what to expect was part of the allure. I not only had a job, but a nice Beamer. Scott needed both to ensure the evening would be a success. And what I mean by "success," well, we didn't even know. Nonetheless, I told him I'd meet him at the club in Pacific Beach.

When I arrived, sure enough, there was Scott seated at a table with four Scandinavian beauties. Everything he said was true. He was smiling like he'd discovered the cure for unhappiness. With his patented suaveness, a real gentleman, he introduced me to the gang, and we went right to the evening at hand. Drinks flowed, there was dancing—mostly the four girls dancing together. All I could do was stare, dumbfounded, amazed that Scott had pulled this off.

It was around 2 A.M. when everyone piled into my car. The Swedes wanted to continue the party at the beach. They brought their enthusiasm, and Scott and I thought we'd somehow done something right to earn this favor with the gods. Straight out of the car, everyone sprinted toward the water. Then, much to my, and our, utter amazement, the girls shed their clothes and frolicked into the surf rolling up the San Diego shoreline. Why Scott and I did not join them in the water, I don't know. Instead, we just stood there—all eyes. Bright, full moon beaming overhead as four Swedish nudes played in the cool water, foreign words drifting up the beach, which soon came closer and closer as water glistened and dripped off their bodies.

What I do know, without doubt, is that when Anna exited the water, all I desired was her body. Always the opportunist back then, but mostly a man, I took off my shirt and gave it to her. But she seemed more interested in finding her clothes than hooking up with me. Still, all I could do was peer deep into the night sky repeating, "Thank you, God."

Anna was most definitely out of my league in all respects. Her most stunning quality—if there is such a thing for a truly beautiful woman—is her green eyes. Then again, her breathtaking body coupled with her dark-brown hair and captivating Swedish attitude toward nudity were equally as magnificent. The evening came to an end at an apartment of one of the girls' friends where a colorful poster of a long-dead Cuban leader hung. Although I had visions of a communal evening of sex, those soon ended, but we had plans to hang out again.

Our entire summer was spent in this fashion—seeming endless trips to the beach—until I finally found the courage to ask Anna out on a real date, just us and a quiet corner table somewhere. Our summer romance turned into a first kiss in a man-made Polynesian garden where large-leafed plants with bright flowers were misted by the waters of the bay.

Eighteen months later, I found myself on a plane to Sweden with Anna to meet her parents. Her father, Voldemar, did not appear overly thrilled to see his daughter on the arm of an American.

One night after a long dinner at a restaurant that Anna's brother Jan had designed, Voldemar enthralled us with his WWII stories, most notably the story of how he and his brother escaped the Russians when they were part of the invasion of Latvia.

"As the sun was rising, we left in a small fishing boat," Voldemar said. "The Russian tanks were rolling in. They were hunting down and killing all the young men. We were out some distance in the water when one tank turned its gun towards our boat—a direct hit was to be our death. But, a miracle happened; a solider popped out of the turret and looked toward us. He lifted his arm and waved, as if to say good luck. He never fired his big gun at us, so that's how my brother and I ended up in Sweden. Once there, I met Siv." It sounded like a story he was used to telling.

After dinner, drinks, cigars and settling of the bill, we ended up in Voldemar's living room. It was late. I was sitting with Anna, and Siv sat at Voldemar's side. We were surrounded by the original oil paintings, drawings and etchings that Voldemar had bought at auctions throughout Europe. I obviously appeared anxious, and Siv just seemed to be waiting for his fireworks. Voldemar began a long speech about his love for Anna. I don't know what overcame me, what power in the universe wanted me to make a fool out of myself, get kicked out of this young woman's family home, or perhaps win big with my bold move. I interrupted him mid-sentence, asking for his permission to marry his daughter. Anna and Siv looked relieved, then shocked. Voldemar was unpredictable, they knew it, and I did not.

Without a word, he walked out of the room. Anna and Siv stared at me—had I totally gone down in flames? Shit!

I followed Voldemar to the kitchen, hoping he'd accept me into his family—this kid he'd just met hours earlier. Once again, I told him how much I loved his daughter and how I wanted to marry her.

"Yes," he said. "But now you must go."

As I headed out of the living room, I asked Anna, "What just happened?"

"You should have just asked him privately, man to man," she explained.

"How was I to know that's how you do it?" I responded, feeling on top of the world, had a tinge of relief because Voldemar had not immediately said no.

"He's that way. I think he likes you, though," Anna said, hoping this encouragement was enough to keep me going.

That all happened some twenty-five years ago. I tend to dwell on all the good memories and bury the bad ones. Maybe we all do that.

Anna is the heart and soul of our house; her love is everywhere. When our family was young, she tried her hardest to keep the peace—running to each cry or question, holding them when they needed it, setting limits to her three-counts, and screaming when she had been pushed to her limits after the fiftieth "no" or some extreme act of stupidity that only young minds can conjure up. But most importantly, Anna's love is always there, and our four children understand that.

I am sort of an inventor, working in medical device research. I can regale you with details of my job—this profession fascinates me at times—but I prefer to read or write when I have some spare time. My real love is being with my wife and kids, doing all I can for them—playing tennis, going out to dinner, hanging out at the pool or helping them with their schoolwork. My life is about being a father. I love playing tennis, and whenever I say, "Tennis," Oliver, our Jack Russell terrier, gets excited and follows my every move, wagging his tail until I get Adam, Hanna, Anna, or someone from the home team, Providence Lake, my last choice—to play. Oliver looks at me until I say, "Let's go," which signals him to jump up into the car.

Adam often played tennis with me, and I loved it when he did. He started playing at age eight. At sixteen, he was a young man with clear eyes and a never-ending smile, going to weekly practices and tournaments, escaping on weekends with me and his sister, Hanna. I sat and watched every stroke as he ran through life. Adam loved to listen to music. He was always dancing around the house with his iPod, his ear-piece plugged into only his right ear, the left ear open so he could hear the world around him. He never took off his yellow LIVE STRONG bracelet—some kind of good-luck charm. He liked to make sure his sisters were protected, but gave them lots of trouble when he wanted to.

Adam was Anna's little boy, and he loved it when she said, "I love you, Adam." And to that he always responded, "I love you, Mama."

At fourteen, Ms. Hanna, our second child, was the princess of the house. She kept her room the cleanest and, and in some ways, was like Flacken the cat. Both fussy.

Hanna slept in her room most afternoons after school. Although she liked her solitude, she was very aware of her surroundings. She played the big-sister role with Ms. Olivia and Ms. Sofia, letting them know she was the eldest and smartest of the girls. She loved art and design, and kept her surreal drawings in a book, sometimes letting others see her creations. Her other big thing was shopping, and she'd go to the mall most anytime. In the same vein, she was a goal-orientated, responsible young lady.

Moreover, if things got scary, by this I mean out of line, with cursing and stomping around the house, I could be sure that Hanna would make a big fuss until all was settled just to her specifications.

Olivia was quite a pushover. Her kindness, generosity, and passion for life were second to none. She was generous and full of a contagious enthusiasm—a soft-hearted, sensitive little girl with big ideas. But she could be more than a little bossy, playing the mother role when she saw something out of line. She especially liked to correct Sofia and me whenever she saw an opportunity. Drop dead beautiful, long hair, curious eyes, she wasn't wearing make-up yet, but it was soon to come. She was and still is very organized. Her desk was always neat—pens and papers all placed in their spots. She collected figurine angels, which were displayed on shelves in her room. She played the violin, but needed to practice more. There's much goodness in her.

Sofia, the baby of the family, knew how to compete for attention. Sofia was cunning and understood how to use her status as the youngest to get her sisters and brother into big trouble by highlighting the broken universal laws that parents believe are the foundation of a peaceful household. Anna and I agree that she was a master at this. She loved the attention and danced around the house, improvising new moves to her playful narrations. I was her primary audience, and her stage was the master bedroom. Sofia played the violin in the school orchestra, following Olivia's lead.

Sofia was afraid of storms; they'd always bothered her. High winds, thunder, and any lightning sent her to our room at night, into our bed for reassurance against harm. She had this strange look about her when the skies darkened. She'd stare out the window or step outside, allowing her meteorological senses to take over—to determine the duration and intensity of the storm. She could sense the sky; any commotion in the weather aroused her suspicions.

Adam was Sofia's protector. She ran to him for sibling love, going downstairs to his room when Hanna and Olivia refused to comfort her.

Sofia's love for Adam was magnified by his protection of her.

3 A New Day

Each morning at the Stephens house in Milton, Georgia, a dog, a cat and a half-naked man start the new day, rain or shine.

You can set your clock to what happens.

As soon as dawn appears on the opaque curtains, the alarm beckons, which causes Oliver to stir, and why not? He is no different than Anna and me when it comes to his desire to continue a peaceful sleep.

But Oliver's protests are to no avail because our cat Flacken meows continuously to let us know it is time to open the door for her.

As I sit up in bed, a bubble rises in the sheets at the foot of the bed and moves toward me; two black eyes soon appear. Oliver slides his head and soft ears against my body and flops down on the sheets, hoping once again to convince me to stay in bed. Again, to no avail.

I get up slowly and snap my fingers. Oliver rises with urgency and strolls to the end of the bed, jumps down, whips his ears back and forth like propeller blades, making a soft fluttering sound, then stretches into a bow of sorts—forepaws forward, head held high, tail twitching. He holds this stance for a moment, then gives me a look that says he's ready to go.

Oliver usually takes the lead, looking back to make sure I'm still there. Pausing at the front door, he waits for it to open, then rushes down the steps and onto the grass. Flacken is sometimes just behind us waiting. If not, she will soon appear.

I look to see where the paper has landed; it is always in

a different place. I guess the speed and toss can never be the same. Of greater importance, however, is why I even subscribe to the *Atlanta Journal-Constitution* in the first place. It's so full of crap.

While I'm contemplating this baffling question, Oliver investigates his toiletry needs, giving a sniff or two before finally lifting his leg to warm some dismayed bush. In underwear and bare feet, I continue my journey down the driveway toward the newspaper, hoping no one drives by.

Bending over to pick it up, I try, without success, to keep my legs straight. My aging knees and tight muscles try to stretch, forcing me to contemplate one of life's truisms: Not only are my joints getting stiffer and stiffer as the years pass by, but I am also feeling pains more frequently during the winter months.

Before I can take myself too seriously, however, I glance toward Oliver, who suddenly appears frozen—left paw slightly up, a statue, as if concealed in some way.

As I walk toward him, I look away, which only encourages his desire to remain motionless. His hope is to astonish me. And as I draw near, he retracts slightly before pouncing forward. I play my role accordingly, acting surprised when he lands at my feet.

Oliver knows how much I love this morning exchange. I always thank him for his efforts and complain if he forgets.

Flacken has joined us. Sometimes she sits on the front porch, watching, as if to say, "What are those two fools doing?" Or sometimes she just walks along, ignoring our morning rumba. She is part of our morning ritual, if only in a small way.

Or maybe she just doesn't care.

4 The Tree House

March 1, 2006

Sitting in a tree house at the edge of our woods, I was surrounded by towering pines and the loving presence of two of my daughters, Olivia and Sofia.

It was the first day of March 2006, and I couldn't think of anywhere else I'd rather be. Perfect setting, perfect weather and perfect company.

My day began in the garden, watching from afar as the sounds of our daughters' laughter rang throughout the forest. Suddenly feeling as if I was missing out on something important, I found myself banging up the ladder leading to the tree house I built with Adam years ago. It's one room with a large, open window looking out over the meadow, with a small balcony. You could climb up a set of nailed-in planks onto the tin roof crow's nest, where you could sit amongst the trees. Sometimes it's okay to have not fully grown up.

On this day Olivia and Sofia were baking mud pies, which cooked ever-so-slowly in the sun's low heat, its glow relaxingly dim. So I just sat there in that tree house, peering out at the soft light as it shadowed the forest's carpet of pine needles.

In short order, Sofia, with her windblown hair and shorts spotted in mud, went below to gather Oliver into her arms. But when she attempted to climb the ladder, she and the dog got stuck. She cried out, "Dad, give us a hand."

My first thought: Four-legged animals shouldn't be in trees.

Then again, what did I know? Far too many years had passed since I viewed life through the eyes of an eight-year-old. Sofia soon climbed back down without a word.

Once Oliver was safe and sound high above, his curiosity took over, and he soon realized the advantages of height. Sitting by my side, as he often did, he looked down, turning his head to each new sight and sound. And then reclining, his ears ever on the alert, Oliver enjoyed the forest's choir. Chirping came from all directions; birds were everywhere.

Soon, Olivia was checking on her mud pies. She was pleased with their progress, and I was happy to just be there with her.

Olivia is my curious one, a great listener—for a twelve-year-old. When she was near, she was always attuned for up-to-the-minute news. And her use of it was her calling card when she saw a need to impose herself, which she did with rapid, paralyzing annotations.

She liked things clean and straight—closed boxes, polished nickels, clean sheets. Puzzles must be completed. She had her unbearable moments, too, where she told you how to do this or that or what not to say. Her demands were meant to bring a conclusion or closure to a situation she felt must be ended—right then and there.

She was a-slammer-of-doors, hiding behind them until her frustration passed. Or, if she felt the need to voice her opinion, she did so and then closed the door.

She was cute as a kitten. Her little nose was highlighted by her smile, which pushed her cheeks out, rounding to little white pillows of perfect skin that shone like two full moons. Her hair was straight and long, with a hint of blonde that darkened over time. Still, I remember when she was dishwater blonde for the first eight years of her life.

Her eyes, clear as the sky, showed an inquisitive happiness most of the time.

As I took time to walk down that memory lane, Sofia returned to the tree house with a handful of white-and-yellow spring daffodils. They had a slight, pleasant smell to them.

She smiled as she placed the flowers in a bamboo vase, then turned to Oliver and said, "I'll be right back, boy. Stay here and don't move."

Knowing her mother was busy in the kitchen cooking, Sofia soon returned with warm cinnamon rolls. Oliver's attention immediately went from bird chirps to Sofia's treats, his tail in a constant wag.

And my attention? Let it suffice that I was touched by Sofia's kindness. It truly was a blessing, for all of us nestled in that tree house at the edge of the woods.

It was where I was meant to be.

5 In Our Garden

One of the reasons I started keeping a journal was to help keep alive the events which bring joy to my life and my family's life. So, with my faithful Oliver at my side, sharing an old wooden bench in the shadows of the tall pines, we both keep a close eye on nature and the children's lives.

Late February 2006: Winter's bitter cold is almost behind us. Its constant breezes keep the sky cloud-free. It is so pleasant to sit in the garden, in the unbroken light. When the crocuses are up, their yellows, whites, and purples are the first signs that winter is not endless.

The tulips and daffodils are newborn—looking toward heaven, eager to begin their life's journey, overflowing with hope.

March 4: It is amazing how instantaneously a garden grows; each day brings new life. The tulips' translucent colors ooze through their new buds; their colorful flames will soon sparkle.

Small shoots are on the trees and hydrangeas; it is the growing season. But the crocuses are fading in numbers. It is sad how they give up. Each morning they open their petals to the sky and close them at night, day after day, until they lay down on the ground, never to rise again.

March 10: A gentle spring rain makes water-beads on the leaves, emerald gems of all sizes. Some are set and some are in flux, gliding down the concave tulip leaves. The first tulip has opened just slightly, recreating its world.

The Bradford pear tree shines brightly, bearing individual white flowers on every branch. The hydrangeas are still skeletons—brown bark hides hanging from their limbs. Soon it will be their day.

The birds sing overhead as Oliver digs in the mud.

March 19: The garden is in full bloom. Thirty-six tulips and most of the daffodils are bright yellow. The grape hyacinths have started to show their purple populace. Flacken, the garden tiger, strolls in the bush, finding a place to hide in the irises. Then, without any notice, she leaps and is gone.

Every year: I cannot forget that the sun is what cultivates the garden. Its rays are absorbed, making the glorious picture. Once, the ground was frozen and bare. After a few short, warm days, beauty comes forth from withered life.

Each year the garden withstands the winter cold and summer heat. Each year it endures for the birds and butterflies.

Any year: When the crocuses are up, their yellows, whites, and purples are the first signs that life is not endless. Here I find circumstances that are greater than all other circumstances, where everything that has life gives us a sign. Thank heaven.

6 Providence (Lake)

April 10, 2006

A large dirt embankment held back the brook's flow. The wind tried hard to blow the small waves to cover the grass along the dam's edge. The shore was irregular, surrounded by hardwoods and pines, each sending a branch or root to drink.

This lake is our neighborhood's most beautiful and expressive feature.

Ducks in pairs, families, and a loner sat on its tranquil surface. The hermit duck always made the most noise. The duck family sat together, minding its own business, a watchful eye on their babies. Time moved slowly, like the fowl on the water. The lake tolerated a loon now and then.

The water is a misty bluish-green color, from the muddy bottom of dark clay sediment. The sun reflects off glassy alcoves or shimmers on the water. Providence Lake has two faces—one calm, the other restless. Weather changes its expression, depending on the wind and light, on this living body.

Sounds added their voices to the tranquil setting—birds sang or chirped, ducks quacked, and occasionally there was the low buzz of a solitary bee. But it was the spring water that made its presence felt most as it escaped through the man-made concrete overflow.

And in the distance was the rumbling of our neighborhood.

Every degree of color shone in the water's reflection. The

rich reds, browns, yellows, and greens were all represented. And in these various colorful impressions, our home's diffused images were reflected as well—despite the best effort of our trees, which pushed forward to conceal the house.

Boat docks litter the water's edge, decaying in its shadows. The lake was calm that evening. Its water transformed in the dusk to a murky, smooth, glossy surface, which softened the moment. The treetops were still, many looking like skeletons. Leafless branches reached out to the coming darkness.

And as I rested on a neighbor's bench my thoughts were with providence—how good comes with the bad, for reasons I thought I'd never understand.

Once Mom kicked my father out of the four-bedroom, upper-middle class, suburban house in late 1970, James, Lynn and I took advantage of the chaos in our own peculiar ways.

Mom got a job at Joe Wilson Realty, mainly for the benefits—which included her new male partners, Ed and John. So skillful was she at climbing the corporate ladder, Mom eventually worked her way into bed with Joe Wilson himself. Not that us kids were overly distraught because the money flowed. Joe owned the business, had a new Cadillac in the lot. He had a big fat wallet and that struck the right chord.

For her own convenience, Mom opened an account at a liquor store adjacent to her office. It was a friendly emporium; not only would they deliver cases of champagne and bottles of Smirnoff to the house with just a phone call, but they also cashed Mom's checks. It was a win-win for all of us. Mom could feed her addiction without lifting a finger, and once she lapsed into a drunken stupor, we'd rifle her purse for spending money.

She started out as a quiet drunk, drinking until she passed out on Sundays, then sobering up by Monday, or sometimes Tuesday. She'd pretend like nothing had happened, using her cunning skills of deceit to convince us it was a weekend illness or some bullshit like that. As time passed, she became more inhuman—had less heart and was less concerned with her reasons. She wanted us to know that we just had to accept her for what she had become, but without openly acknowledging it to her. So, we began not to love her—fell out of love with her. Things got to where she could not convince us that she deserved any degree of respect. But still she was "our mother"— the alcoholic—our alchoholic.

Family entertainment was our weekly excursion to a nearby Safeway. It was there that Mom stocked up on orange juice, her mixer of choice. My brother, sister and I piled food into the shopping carts, which Mom interpreted as our "weekly treat."

All in all, we became quite adept at raising ourselves, but still Mom hired Yolanda, a wonderful Spanish woman from Tijuana, who lived with and cared for us Monday morning through Friday afternoon. She was our replacement mother who couldn't speak English. She must have been in her twenties, Catholic, I guess, from the cross she kept in her room. She was a good woman, did all she could to fill in the missing parts—making meals, being there when we got home from school, patching the worn out knees in our pants, making a middle class home in suburbia, a life that she herself never could have afforded. To my mother, Yolanda was always second class. I didn't see it that way; she was raising us even though it was only for a short while.

Of course Mom's ulterior motive for hiring Yolanda was that it permitted her to stay out late with her men, which Mom termed "working hard to put a roof over our heads."

Yolanda was a saint. In no time at all, we clearly understood her short list of rules, all of which were given in Spanish. I can still hear her quelling our bickering with words that we could barely make out through her thick accent: "Don't hit Lynn."

Yolanda left after around three years. She must have had better opportunities or had saved some money so she could be with her family, and with her went what sense of order or normalcy we'd accumulated. Chaos reigned by the time I entered high school in 1973. Making matters worse, Mom was drowning heavily in the booze, and money was running low. No longer could we steal from her to sustain ourselves. So, it was time for an expansion of revenue.

At first I tried my hand at a newspaper route, but this required a supplementary income because it only netted me fifty dollars a month—not nearly enough to sustain high school-type habits. But opportunity knocked when it finally dawned on me that, due to Mom now disappearing for entire weekends at a time, I could put our house to work for us.

The parties started on a small scale—our only expense, the cost of a keg of beer. But like all innovative businesses, we grew as the demand for our services increased. In no time at all, our house became the high school version of Animal House—we could supply whatever our patrons desired, behind the locked bathroom doors were the sounds of sex, moans heard between songs. The parties grew to include live bands and security, not to mention exclusive by-invitation-only access—unless, of course, you happened to be a drop-dead-beautiful girl or John Belushi.

Along with the risks and rising costs came a price increase for admittance. By this time we were clearing $500 each weekend, plus whatever money my sister Lynn pocketed—although she was only ten, she was light-years ahead of her time when it came to enterprise. She'd simply walk among the party-goers and ask for money. No one refused her.

Mom's return to the family homestead on Sunday afternoons was without incident. Granted, the house reeked of beer, but she never asked. The only time fear entered the picture was when one of our "customers" inadvertently sat on an antique marble table that Mom had inherited. We repaired it and held our collective breath, no retribution ever came. That's when I knew she had lost all sense of the world around her, most importantly any sense of her home or her personal space. It was at this point that we knew we had complete control of the house.

Besides the booze, Mom's drug of choice was downers, which she got from our family doctor—a quack who was later arrested for some sexual act with himself in a public bathroom. Her standard prescription was ten Quaaludes; she'd drive my brother and me to the pharmacy, and we'd run in and get the prescription filled. No big deal, they knew us after awhile. But this ended when she added a zero to the prescription, sending us in to pick up "100 Ludes." "They don't prescribe in this quantity," the pharmacist looked disturbed, as he picked up the phone to make a call.

My brother and I had never run so fast in our lives, exiting the pharmacy and jumping into the car—yelling for Mom to haul ass, that her sick plan had just backfired. Of course, it wasn't her fault; her delinquent kids got the blame for the additional zero added to the script. I learned early what it was like to be framed.

After the drugstore incident, we knew that any future prescriptions we brought in would be closely scrutinized. We didn't need or want that kind of heat. But the good news was that I discovered I had a buddy whose father was a pharmacist; the kid somehow masterminded a drug heist, then showed up at our house with bags full of prescription drugs—thousands of uppers and downers in assorted colors, but none of them in marked bottles. We solved that problem by acquiring a PDR (*Physician's Desk Reference*), educated ourselves on the various product lines and went into inventory control, marketing and distribution.

Just like that, we were rolling in money. We became "Lucy in the Sky with Diamonds" without the marshmallow pies or Mr. Kite and the Walrus. That would come later.

Mom became one of our best customers. We explained to her that a friend's dad, a pharmacist, was the source. She didn't care; it was just supply and demand at that point. We'd quickly fill her order, especially when we needed her heavily medicated or totally passed out. Hell, we once had a party with her properly dosed and locked in her bedroom.

This is not to suggest that I was void of all moral principles—sure I'd pass along some drugs, but I had my standards. Despite a houseful of "easy" high school party girls, I was a one-woman man. But even this sort of monogamous affection had a fuzzy detachment to it. I'm speaking of my first high school girlfriend. Her name was Laura, and she was my first serious relationship. It was convenient that she was the next door neighbor's daughter. We would sneak out at night and take a roll in a sleeping bag on the side lawn, and no one ever knew the better. We did it all for about eight years. Got married, then divorced a few months later. Our divorce was inevitable, but hastened along by Laura's pet dog.

My then-wife was adamant about taking the dog for a walk—a two-hour walk and on most Friday nights, no less. Both she and the canine would return home seeming slightly sexually stimulated.

Not being a complete fool, I followed her one night. She got as far as the next-door neighbor's house, than brazenly stepped through his front door. An agonizing peek through the neighbor's bedroom window confirmed she was fucking him. Seeing it like that, made the follow-up so much easier, leaving her and the dog was easy, but I had one more thing to do that night.

I was immersed in amazement and anger, mostly amazement, then mostly anger, then both at the same time, but I was thinking clearly. Up to that moment I'd gotten by on guile—cutting corners, deception, breaking almost every rule set before me. Not that any of that bothered me. After all, I'd convinced myself, I was a product of a dysfunctional home. So I called her father, waited the ten minutes it would take him to arrive. Then I knocked on her lover's door with a roll of quarters in my fist. I beat him. Our dog was barking as Laura pulled my hair, then I just stopped, as her father walked up. I left the three of them together, two standing, one slumped. I left the neighborhood, her father's head hanging low as I drove past them to go check into a hotel.

It was time for me to bail on this lifestyle, to get my act together—clear my head and heart, and begin living a reputable life.

The real healing would only come years later, when I met my Anna.

7 Oliver

June 1, 2007

When he moved in, Anna would call him to her side. The dog always heeded her commands, and Oliver became one of Anna's little babies for the next six months. He liked to sleep in her arms, and they would snuggle together in our bed all the time.

To this day, Oliver still sleeps there, although he does get kicked around more than usual. It was from Anna's Scandinavian warmth that Oliver learned to be kind, loving, and watchful. I know Oliver dwells on this, he must. He doesn't miss getting smacked with the paper during his housetraining or all those long flea showers, or the day he got his nuts hacked off in the vet's office.

At first I was not sure about Oliver. I thought he would be nothing more than a lame-brain nincompoop—just some four-legger who was tripping me on my way to the fridge or sniffing me awake when I fell asleep on the couch, but we grew into great friends. Nowadays, I try not to kick him when he's in the bed, but if I do, he growls until he's acknowledged. We get up together each morning. He has his day; I have mine. His day involves being served his meals and sleeping, while mine is work, so he can catch up on his beauty sleep.

He sits beside me—my faithful friend—at the community pool, where dogs are not allowed, but where some are loved (and snuck in). Of course, Oliver is aware of this and plays it up—big time. He possesses excellent hearing, keen eyesight, continuous energy, a quick mind, and a loving heart.

His tenacity and focus is ever present in his character, with a sacrificing loyalty inherent in his spirited temperament. A quiet restlessness emanates from him, until he dashes away in pursuit of the elusive smells and sounds that call him to action—so amusing for those of us who care to watch.

Oliver's human-like emotion is reflected in his black eyes when he looks into ours, hoping to ensure companionship. He expresses his demeanor in the wag or stillness of his tail. He uses his forepaws like hands, hugging and extending his touch carefully. His movement notifies us of his excitement—from a slow stroll, to his pounce or his prancing horse-like trot. He watches over us from a distance, ears up to monitor our activity, but settles back as we arrive. He acts rapidly if he feels we require his protection. He sleeps with ease, giving an occasional grumble when kicked. But he is always listening, just in case something requires his attention.

His sadness is evident when we leave. He rebels by eating Hanna's underwear, turning over bathroom trash cans, then positions himself in the best place to watch the street, Olivia's upstairs alcove window. His joy is limitless upon our return, we could see him in the window just for a moment, then he disappears. As the door opens, we find him there greeting us with overwhelming love because he knows he is part of our family.

8 Four States, Two National Parks & Elvis

June 8, 2007

I have an appreciation for nature and a need to connect my family's inner world to these outside worlds. We connected the two as we traveled, seeing the world with each other—united and grounded in family. I found these new worlds with them. As a father, I wanted to be their conduit in these adventures—or a sort of a guide—but at the same time, wanted us all to discover together. And so we traveled, and as we walked and moved in and through these places, our love increased, and we discovered not just places, not just tourist spots, but each other.

When we set out, I had no idea how these journeys would turn out. At first they were just vacations—trips to national parks, to Thanksgiving with friends, to Anna's Scandinavia where all the children were baptized in the endless summer's sun. I learned later, while writing this actually, fundamental things about my children—their love for each other, their approaches to and views of each new adventure, their desires to live fully, and their voices, which were so present in our travels, but not simply the sound of their voices, something more, something about who they were as individuals beyond myself and Anna.

Route planned, reservations confirmed, bags packed—we were about to embark on a six-day road trip—one of those frustrating, yet priceless sojourns, where the novelty that is family interaction is guaranteed—given all that time in the car.

We left Oliver and Flacken with the neighbors and hit the road in early morning, loading into the Suburban to begin our drive to Kentucky's Mammoth Caves National Park. Of course, we all needed patience and a high level of tolerance for a trip like this. The car felt packed—way too tight, no elbow room, which required frequent stops. That's how we ended up in Nashville, having breakfast at the Grand Ole Opry. To everyone's disappointment, however, it was way too early to see the concert hall, so we all voted to finish our drive north. Shortly thereafter, the bellyaching began.

"When are we going to get there?" Olivia whined.

"Yeah, I'm tired of being in this car," moaned Adam.

Looking at the GPS, I knew we had at least an hour of hell to go. Not too bad considering how far we'd come. Cautiously I replied, "I don't know. Soon. Around lunch."

"That's over an hour more," complained Hanna, staring out the window. "It's not even eleven o'clock yet."

"Where's the candy?" asked Sofia.

Hanna blurted, "You ate it all…already."

Sofia reached forward for a Coke from the cooler, but Olivia pushed her back into the seat, saying, "Stay on your side."

"Stop touching me."

I took a breath and concentrated on the road. My nerves started to jangle.

"Turn up the radio," Olivia said.

Hanna reached between the seats and turned a couple of knobs. Country music blared through the Suburban.

Adam snapped, "No, not that one—change it."

Before Hanna could touch the knob again, Anna tried to calm everyone by lowering the volume and turning to a preset she thought everyone could live with.

"Oh, not that stuff." Adam put on his iPod and tuned us out to Blink 182.

All four kids grew more hysterical. They fumed, squabbled, and yelled at each other. I wanted to scream, but that was no lesson to teach them. I held it in and tried to concentrate on the fenced bluegrass countryside, but the sounds in the car distracted me.

Sofia shrieked—my heart jumped into my throat. I looked in the rearview mirror.

Was she dying?

"Olivia kicked me," Sofia screamed. "Her feet are dirty."

My racing heartbeat slowed when we finally reached the park sign. We arrived at the Kentucky lodge, all I could say was, "Thank God that's over." Such a frantic connection—or was it? Still, it was concentrated time—it was a start.

We checked into the two rooms we'd reserved months earlier. Both rooms were on the first floor and adjacent to one another. They were small, clean, with outside terraces—a place to be quiet, sit, watch nature, listen to birds, read, write, or just do nothing—everything kids of that age love to do, right?

Hanna, Sofia, and I settled in one room—Hanna vowed to keep it clean—while Adam, Olivia, and Anna took the other. Although the rooms were not connected by an inside door, they could be easily accessed through the terraces' sliding glass doors—the rusted rollers of which announced their opening and closing, signaling the kids were on the move.

We don't travel light, which required me to move all the crap from the car to the rooms. The kids took their own bags, but the rest of the moving was left to me. When the transfer was complete, we walked on the wooden boardwalk to the ranger station.

After we picked up our tickets, a ranger loaded about twenty of us onto a bus and dropped us off at a wooded foothill, where another ranger led us up a footpath to where a concrete bunker protruded from the earth. A heavy, steel door hung within a metal frame below a light. The ranger pulled out his keys and unlocked it. With a swing of the door, the cave's cool air came rushing at us.

Slowly, we descended a flight of metal stairs and were greeted by swarms of insects clinging to the passageway's concrete walls; even more were stuck to the ceiling. We continued our descent. The stoneflies, crickets and dragonflies kept us company with their buzzing. We must have descended at least a hundred steps and passed thousands of bugs before we landed on the cave's dirt floor.

In single file, we turned corner after dark corner, I kept one eye on the low, stone ceilings to avoid hitting my head, the other I focused on the passageway, which gradually opened into the largest cave structures on the continent.

Little Sofia was scared and hung close by. "I don't like this cave," she said. "Can we go back to the rooms?"

Hanna complains about almost everything: "It's dirty. There are too many bugs; one landed on me. The air stinks, I can't breathe. This sucks. Let's get out of here."

Adam found fun right away, as a boy in a cave should, running around, looking at this, touching that.

Anna and I were not sure if Olivia was interested or not. She just seemed to take it all in. Her quiet manner shows itself when she's not sure about something.

This underworld was so separated from the life above. The caverns, carved from waters long gone, were filled with damp, cool air. Rivers ran deep below, taking the earth with their flow. The only light was man-made, and without it, there was perfect darkness to which your eyes could never adjust. You couldn't see your hand in front of your face. You could only feel the remnants behind and in front of you, where people once lived in these earthen hollows for protection, to hide and escape in the darkness of the walls.

The caves resonated with deep isolation. I could only hear steps, breathing, and the occasional echoes of dripping water seeping from the cracks in the ceilings. These are the sounds of confinement. This shadowy solitude would cause me to go crazy, to go numb. My thoughts would fail in this confusion of confinement and depressing darkness that would leave me desolate in God's silence.

There, where I heard the sounds of night as well as the cries of dawn, nature spoke deeply. Our borrowed journey through the underworld took us back to the ranger station gift shop, where the kids seemed at ease. Olivia found a national park passport book.

"Can I get this, Daddy?" she asked with that look to which I can never say no.

Olivia began turning the pages and found the spot for her first national park stamp. Her joy was obvious; she quickly fell in love with the book's organization and orderliness. My reaction: This could be something for us to share for a long time. Although I didn't say it right then, it was a thought that stuck with me that entire trip. I was making plans.

We retreated to our rooms. Anna, Adam, Hanna, and Sofia all took naps, while Olivia and I sat together—turned each page of her new book, looked at the pictures and talked about what national park we should visit next.

"Look, Olivia, the Grand Canyon, Yellowstone. Here's Yosemite, remember we went there?"

It was just her and me, dreaming about the places we had to go, wondering how many we could visit together. I wondered how long this simple moment would last before she grew up and pulled away, like all children do at some point. But not that day. That day we were there doing what fathers and children do, just playing it out together.

We sat there for hours, until the early evening arrived.

As the day's heat subsided, we had dinner at the lodge, where we discovered we were in a dry Kentucky county. One of our family traits was that we, meaning Anna and I, sometimes want/require/enjoy a drink. We had wine in the room, thought about getting it, until we looked around to see the Sunday sober on all the faces in the restaurant. We had no choice. Sodas.

THE NEXT DAYS

Anna and I got out of bed early the next morning, and took a walk in the neighboring hills, a peaceful togetherness parents don't get that often. The park's boardwalk ended at a trail, and nearby was an old graveyard surrounded by a white picket fence.

Carved on one sad headstone was the date of death: June 15, 1857. A slave named Stephen Bishop was buried there. He was employed as a guide and was said to know the caves like no one else. We bowed our heads.

Later, hiking down a progression of paths to the bottom of the hill, we were wowed by the multitude of hardwoods, not to mention the occasional deer, blue herons and sandpipers. Reaching our destination, we found groundwater that surfaced to form a river grotto. The water was a blue-green, rich in minerals. A massive rock hung above the grotto opening. At its low point, a narrow waterfall fell into aquamarine water and flowed into the Green River, which was low that day; tree trunks lined its muddied banks.

It was there that Anna and I sat, listened to a woodpecker work hard for his breakfast. We tried to count the hammerings, to find contentment in the sloshing of the river and each other's un-brushed morning hair. We didn't say much. We both seemed taken aback by nature's revelations. We mentioned the kids, wondered if they were awake, then fell back, silent, into the scenery. Just being together on mornings such as that one assured me of the simple pleasures we could all share as a family, but during this particular moment, we sat and shared its silence. Then we returned to check up on the kids.

Olivia was the first to rise that morning. She was a bit grumpy to find nature so close. Adam was still sound asleep, a blanket in hand, holding it against his cheek. He was still a little boy in so many ways, though sixteen.

After opening the sliding glass door, letting the light in, and banging around in the bathrooms, I announced: "It's time to get up. Your mother and I already took a hike. Come on. Get up."

"No. Let me sleep. What's the rush?" Adam asked.

"Breakfast will be over soon, and it smells so good," I suggested to my always-hungry son.

After breakfast I managed to talk everyone into a second expedition into the Native Americans' ancient tombs. Their gypsum and arrowheads were followed by Europeans, then miners who dug for gunpowder during the Civil War, and each left behind some scattered remnant of their histories. Just the thing I'd like to think that we were doing there as a family. We hiked down a zigzag trail to a large opening in the earth.

Water streamed from the rocks above. Bats flew in the cave.

A ranger told us, "These tunnels stretched over 365 miles, carved by millions of years of descending waters, but today you'll walk and crawl just two miles."

We passed through a massive opening within the earth this time. Within 200 yards we were standing in a grand underground room, which seemed much larger than any man-made auditorium. Its ceiling was ominous; high overhead hung massive limestone rocks, which seemed as if they would come crashing down at any moment. I felt our own insignificance.

As the room narrowed, up ahead there appeared to be a large stone coffin—its lid just open and tilted toward a constricted passageway that descended into a crawl space so low and restricted, the kids' curiosity was heightened. In short order, our children were on all fours, directly in front of Anna and me. And that's when one of them shouted, "How are you gonna fit, Papa? You're gonna get stuck!"

Although I was a little taken aback, I knew it was all in fun. After all, maybe the voice from in front of me was right.

Nonetheless, I managed to navigate the opening, and crawl through the darkness, crossing a bottomless pit that seemed to drop all the way to hell. We continued into domed towers, sloping rock rooms inhabited by transparent salamanders. It was a place of grandeur that only nature could construct.

The kids had a blast. Sofia's fear turned to curiosity, and

Hanna's dissatisfaction and simulated suffering gave way to playful happiness. Olivia seemed to be recording it all for future reference, while Adam had fun taking it in, seeing beauty while continuing to discover his own independence.

Of course, Anna and I were mesmerized by the underground beauty and the kids' sudden change of heart. The cool, windless air and muffled quietness seemed to have a captivating effect on all of us.

On Sunday I woke early to catch the French Open finals. The room's limited channels were on some sort of satellite system, so I convinced the hotel manager how important this match was, and she adjusted the satellite dish so I could watch from the lobby. I was proud of myself.

But then Olivia, Sofia and Hanna came by on their way to the gift shop.

"Dad, that's on the TV in our rooms," they told me. And with that, my bubble burst. But, I hustled to find Adam lying on the bed, his eyes riveted to the TV. Together we watched Nadal win his third consecutive French Open title, both of us wondering if some day Adam would play with such skill. I could see Adam admired this man's strength, stamina and ability with a little disappointment, which my overpowering tennis demands had likely brought on him. I could see Adam wanted to be playing that match for me. I pushed too much, but I couldn't see it then. That realization came much later when Adam called me "The Tennis Nazi." That's when I realized my approach and dreams were not his, and that I'd burned him out on the tennis court those last two years in high school.

Later that morning we packed up and soon on the road— this time to Yellville, Arkansas, and the Buffalo River National Park. I had read about the old cabins built by the CDC above the river, where virgin waters were isolated by the Ozark Mountains, a place I knew nothing about.

The drive to our cabin at the Buffalo Point Concessions

was a true adventure—the quintessential family outing, which I was sure parents nationwide were familiar with: Wrong turns, endless bathroom stops, kids yelling, and the father's insistence to keep moving despite the lack of clear directions. After all, I didn't want to arrive in the middle of the night. I was hoping the family would thank me later.

But as we pulled up to the cabin at 1 A.M., I could only smile to myself. Only under circumstances such as those could intimate domestic disharmonies be so unconsciously passed down from generation to generation, all in the name of "family time." This was character building at its finest.

We got up later than usual the next day, all of us still a bit weary from the night's seemingly endless drive. We strolled to the café, a building perched high on a hill, which overlooked the Buffalo River. A stream snaked along the mountain's edge, light glittering off the faceted surface, as if the water was made of cut gems gleaming. We enjoyed the view of the meandering river and the light show while having eggs and bacon. The sun was shining, the air was fresh—a good day to be on the river.

We stopped at the ranger station first, Olivia wanted to get her book stamped. She took it in, checked the stamp to be sure the date was correct, then stamped the book carefully. I watched with a smile on my face. She looked at me and handed me the book for my inspection. Pleased, we got back in the car and headed toward the docks.

I'd arranged for a nine-mile rafting trip. And with a cache of snacks and bottled water, we were off on a voyage down our country's first designated national river—150 miles in length and free of dams, this Buffalo River flows through the Ozarks.

Although our crew had many captains, just like our drive in, we eventually settled into a rowing team, three per side, yet our strokes were still just a bit in contention with one another's. We gathered a rhythm as if we had a coxswain appear, each stroke gathering speed. We soon mesmerized ourselves with high bluffs, hardwood forests, small islands, and river-rock beaches. The water was clear, its bottom lined with smooth rocks of gold, white, browns, and grays—every earth tone was clear and distinct from the others. Their surfaces shimmered in the calm waters, giving off a sparkle and shine as we moved above them.

We landed on a rock beach, every stone arranged and worn smooth by river water. The stones protested as I walked on them, each readjusting underfoot. Soon a rock-skipping contest broke out, and everyone looked for the perfect rock. This was by no means an easy task. There were many to choose from. Each of us searched for that flat, round rock. And once we found it, we shared our rock-throwing expertise with the others. Every skip counted.

"One, two, three, four, five, six!" we yelled as Anna's rock skipped along its merry way.

Everyone took a turn. And once we were done, we tallied the skips. It was obvious who the winner was. Anna and her rock-slinging methodology were superior. Her record for the day was nine skips on a single throw.

Feeling the heat, in more ways than one, it was time to get back on the river. We launched from our stony island with our new skipper, Anna, taking not only all the children, but also several handfuls of rocks. Shortly thereafter, all of us were in need of cooling off again, so we found a shallow sandbar and jumped in. Anna, Adam, and Sofia were in and out, while Olivia clung to the raft's ropes. Only Hanna sat cooling off in the river—cooling off, that is, until she saw our raft drift away with everyone but her on it.

"Don't sit out there too long, or we could be gone," I said to her.

With a newfound sense of urgency, she raced through the water toward the raft. Her sudden drop into deep water didn't deter her determination to reunite. There was no panic; she had a calm, resolved look on her face as she swam to us and boarded the raft.

Olivia was still holding on with all her strength when I

pulled her aboard. She looked relieved to be rescued. "Thanks! I thought you forgot about me."

"Never," I told her.

We continued down the river. We saw a deer nearby, its head above the river's surface, moving against the current. Turtles jumped off rocks and swam below as hawks flew overhead. For the most part, we had the river almost to ourselves. We came across only four other adventurers the entire day.

Hunger, coupled with the exertion of rowing under a hot sun, started to take its toll. Although we had done our best to ration our food and water, our supplies seemed light. The culprit? We believed it was Anna, who not only had been secretly eating most of the Corn Nuts, but also picked out the M&M's from the trail mix. But like all worthy captains, she stoutly denied the accusations with such clarity and force, that she was able to stifle the crew's M&M mutiny by the mere force of her strong will.

On our way back to the cabin, we drove through the settlement of Rush, a ghost town. Its wooden structures were abandoned more than a hundred years ago—houses with wood porches, overhung with sagging rafters, and bleached from years of sun and rain. The forest's overgrowth shaded the town whose surrounding hills were once said to be laden with gold and silver ore. We slowed down, took in the town's desertion: It had a feeling of loss, nothing we wanted to step into.

Thus, our great Buffalo River excursion had an ending. I wanted to come back to this place, ride that river again, only older to see the new channels, its eddy currents that captured the woody remains. I made a reservation that I knew we were unlikely to keep because desire is not always a reality.

On our drive home to Georgia, we stopped in Memphis to visit Graceland. Along the road it seemed as though every Elvis commercial opportunity had been taken advantage of. But once we stepped foot onto his private property, the might and majesty of the King of Rock and Roll overwhelmed us.

But what thrilled me the most was that, even though I

was sure our children must have known, in some way, Elvis by name and reputation, they got to see first-hand how he lived with his fame and family—the house, the planes, the clothes, the jewelry. It was impossible for me to not to feel an emotional tie to Elvis, his music playing non-stop while I walked his footsteps up the path.

We spent the last night of our journey in Nashville and arrived home the next morning. Oliver and Flacken were waiting for us at the door. Flacken gave us a cat lecture while Oliver jumped all over us.

9 The Blue Ridge & Great Smokey Mountains

July 9, 2007

We arrived for a three-day stay at the Pisgah Inn, a lodge in the Blue Ridge Mountains, and checked into two upstairs rooms. The lodge sat atop a mountain with impressive views. Its dining room was rustic and had huge picture windows through which we could enjoy the mountains' grandeur. That was exactly what we did while waiting for dinner. We enjoyed soft drinks and wine in our rocking chairs, while the evening light settled with a deep purple on the mountains, which sat far in the distance and were framed by the giant single-paned windows.

After a meal of country meats and vegetables, we retreated to our rooms: Adam, Sofia, and me in one; Hanna, Olivia, and Anna in the other. With only a few TV channels, we entertained ourselves by discussing sleeping arrangements. We had no method to our madness, it was more based on bed size and who would fit where and with whom at any given moment.

Adam, sixteen and looking more like a man, stared at Sofia with his big-brother look. "Can you sleep with Papa tonight? I've gotta have my own bed, they look small." It wasn't so much a need for separation from Sofia, but Adam had a need for breathing room. New freedoms were on every horizon for him.

Little Sofia wanted to sleep with Adam, but was tired. She looked at me, then Adam, saying with weary eyes, "Well, Papa, I guess it's you and me. Adam doesn't want me."

I knew Sofia preferred cuddling with her big brother, but she was stuck with me.

Tucked in for the night, Adam asked, "Why are hotel pillows always so flat? They all are the same at these damn national lodges."

My reply, "Yeah, you're right. Not comfortable at all."

Sofia cackled at the pillow observation as she tested their flatness.

"That's why you should always bring your own," Adam added, flipping through the TV channels a couple more times. "These are lousy selections."

We talked and joked about nothing in particular—a family at rest.

Just as Adam's eyes grew heavy, his blanket snuggled to his cheek, he said good-night to Sofia and me, then clicked the TV off. After a moment of absolute silence, he was asleep.

Sofia and I arranged and rearranged pillows and blankets. Next thing I knew the morning light cut through our curtained windows.

I woke up first and saw a heavy fog running along the sunlit pinnacles. Opening the sliding glass door, I was greeted by fresh, cool air. From our porch, the trees were so close that I could reach out and cause a shower below since dewdrops coated every leaf.

Anna heard my moving about through the thin walls and came out on her porch with coffee. Because our rooms weren't joined, she opened the outside hallway door to let me in to get a cup for myself. Her room was dark; Olivia and Hanna were asleep in their tidy-orderly sort of way, which required Hanna to have her own bed, too—something she always tried to make happen on our trips.

Anna and I stepped onto the porch, enjoyed the morning sunlight sitting together, drinking her hotel-concocted, practically undiluted coffee—she always insists on it being strong. The wooden chairs creaked as we gazed at the miles of mist-covered mountains.

I'd picked up a trail map earlier and had it with me and worked to sell Anna on what was becoming our morning togetherness. We walked the trail and talked to each other, which was like stealing time from the past. We didn't say much: "How'd you sleep?" "The coffee tastes great." "What should we do today?" Soon we were off on our morning hike. Because of the high elevation, we were breathing hard. Nonetheless, the surrounding beauty of plain, pure nature pulled us along. Our care for each other grew, and we seemed to recall something from our past on that walk with each stress or slip on the trail.

Through dewey paths that glistened with water-laden leaves, we continued our journey up a small ridge. It was early summer, and the rhododendrons, azaleas, and mountain laurel were thriving. We walked along rock outcrops and under shaded pines that opened to meadows, each sprinkled with wildflowers. The two of us were released in those mountain hours. I thought of making love to Anna, but never acted on it, but should have, no one was there. It was nice to think about and is nice to think about now, still thinking on that desire as I write this.

Our morning ended when our thoughts turned to our sleeping children back at the lodge. We reversed our journey, worried they might be awake and wondering where we were. It was hard to leave the kids, some innate sense of parenting, I guess. But once back at our rooms, the kids were still asleep. Anna and I made our usual morning noises, and the kids finally woke. The Great Smokey Mountains were close—too close to ignore. Our drive took us along roads fitted into the Appalachian landscape, where stacked-wood fences, massive, stone tunnels and meadows extended along the countryside. We arrived at a visitor's center, where an old farmhouse, mill, barn, and working sheds were preserved. Along the farm's dirt road sat a fenced pen, where pink pigs dug the dirt with their snouts as they grunted at one another. By the side of the road ran a crooked creek, and the trees that lined the creek and road provided shade and cool places to rest or get wet.

A large bolder, rounded from years of erosion, sat in the water just far enough out to discourage most, but it invited us to reach it. Olivia was quick to take advantage, braving the weak-willed current, claiming her stone island free of brothers and sisters. Adam also soon invaded. That left four of us on the creek's bank. Hanna was next. She climbed a tree that hung over the water and dropped. Sofia watched her brother and sisters, but followed Hanna's playful direction to the tree, then the creek. Anna and I sat together in the shallows and watched the kids.

We could only smile. Loving them, yes, and not the least bit surprised by their beauty.

There was a mist on these waters and mountains, which seemed to be everywhere. The haze raced to fall, like a ghost was evaporating to someplace greater, fog settling in low places allowing only mountain tops to rise above.

That late afternoon, our drive took us along the paved road where a fast-moving river rolled over the river rocks. We stopped to fish with the poles we brought from home. In short order, Adam lost one of his shoes to the current, but then somehow managed to catch it with his cast and hook. It didn't take long for me to get a pole in the water, too. There we were, father and son, casting lines here and there, trying to appear as if we actually knew what we were doing while reassuring each other there were, indeed, plentiful fish in the river. Of course, the girls ignored us as they splashed.

Adam and I looked at each other, and without further hesitation, we dropped our poles and jumped in. Soon, one of the kids made use of a strong current, which carried her along at a solid pace—a downstream V which dropped her into a deep pool. We rode this watercourse over and over, until the evening dusk and mountain chill settled in, which called us back to the warmth of the car.

Back at the lodge, the kids ran off somewhere, and the sun was an orange sphere dropping off the edge of the earth. Anna and I sat together, drinking beers, rocking the chairs, wondering and watching the slow decline of light as we found a sense of peace, a warm glow as we gazed as far as the eye could see at blue-green peaks. Those ghost-mists settled into the valleys, while mountaintops stood tall and fading into darker blues.

Our three-day stay had a multitude of pluses and few minuses. On the debit side, I watched Roger Federer win his fifth Wimbledon title. Don't ask me why—especially where there were so many better ways to spend my time.

But whatever dysfunction I caused by my tennis addiction or my demands to not let our summer come to a close may have caused, it was overshadowed by being surrounded and embraced by family—my wife, a son and three beautiful daughters—in the mountains, alongside a river that ran through them.

And as a bonus, Olivia's stamp book continued to grow with the addition of two more national park stamps and one state park.

10   The Cloisters in New York

July 10, 2007

Following the business meetings of the day, a twenty-dollar cab ride took me through New York Upper West Side along the waters to a silent place from another time.

Along the Hudson River, atop a small hill, sits The Cloisters. Built from twelfth- and fourteenth-century European Christian artifacts, John D. Rockefeller, Jr., reconstructed this New York abbey. His need to create such a place not only illustrates his ability to reposition history, but also his obliging desire to establish tranquility in this city of finance and capitalism.

Men and their money, they'll do the strangest things—some give, but most won't. My father taught me, inadvertently, his confusing lesson about how not to waste money. What money meant to him is something I'll never forget.

Dad didn't know it, but it would be his last year in the house, his last shot with his family and as the father at the 4228 Mars Way address.

Whenever I approached my dad and asked for anything out of the ordinary, he'd drop his favorite cliché on me: "A penny saved is a penny earned." Because I couldn't buy anything with a penny, I always reached for the moon—dollars.

When The Beatles' *Let It Be* album hit record stores in the early 1970s, my mother got caught up in our generation's revolution and bought a Beatles poster, which hung on my bedroom wall. The poster had this mystical freedom. All it took was one glimpse of their carefree way of life, the four of them sporting their free-flowing hair like a badge of honor—and I wanted to be just like them.

Mom had no problem with it. After all, she'd embraced her own concept of freedom years earlier. In her inebriated state of mind, wearing flower-patterned, hippie dresses naturally went hand-in-hand with her screwdrivers. My mop-top hairstyle either stroked her vanity or served as a needle jabbed directly into my father's somber demeanor.

If I had to make book on it, I'd chose the latter. After all, he was permanently locked into the 1950s—flat-top hair style, white shirts, dark slacks, white socks and penny loafers. He had the look of an all-American engineer, which he was, working at Convair, helping build the first stage of the ICBM rockets. An impressive job, yes. But to my way of thinking, he was a man who woke up one day only to find himself on a different planet; he must have felt that fear of loss coupled with his empty belief in nothingness after death. He was witnessing social transformation, free love, rock and roll. You wore your thoughts of rebellion with your hair, flowered polyester shirts, flashing peace signs and "the finger." His family was embracing all of it, and he took it as a form of betrayal. It went against everything he knew, defied his grand narrative.

Nonetheless, he wasn't about to give in without a fight, he was one of those that could not accept the change that was happening all around.

I was eleven when Dad decided to teach me his lesson of giving and receiving. Knowing I wanted money for candy and to do the kinds of things that kids want to do, Dad said, "If you get a haircut, I'll give you five dollars."

Being a kid, my response was, "Okay, but can I have it now?"

"I'll pay you after the haircut—let's go."

We jumped into Dad's Volkswagen Bug and drove to his barbershop. When we got there, a gentleman was already in the chair, a white towel wrapped around his face while, with precise gliding movements, the barber sharpened his straight-razor on a leather strap.

Dad stepped forward and said, "Can you fit my son in today? His mother let his hair get too long."

The barber looked at my hair and grinned. "Sure. Just give me about ten minutes, Mr. Stephens." I knew the man was thinking he couldn't wait to cut that hippie's hair off.

Ten minutes? Good grief. I'd have to wait an eternity with nothing to do except thumb through boring, year-old magazines. Ah, but what the heck—at ten-cents apiece, five bucks meant fifty candy bars.

Dad whispered to the barber specific instructions before I climbed into the red leather and chrome chair. He wrapped a strip of fine tissue paper around my neck and followed that with a blue-and-white striped smock, which he draped over my chest and shoulders.

A click of a switch, then the buzz of the clippers as they glided across the top and sides of my head. Hair fell onto my lap. Lots and lots of hair.

I moved my hand from beneath the smock, and took hold of a handful of my shorn locks and, with an agonized heart, rubbed them between my thumb and forefinger.

I turned to see my reflection, and there was my dad looking back at me in the mirror. Gone was my "Let It Be" look, replaced with my father's flat-top.

My immediate reaction? "I sure as hell won't be doing this again."

My secondary reaction was to jump out of the chair, turn to Dad and say, "A deal's a deal. Can I have the five bucks now? I want to go next door to the 7-Eleven."

Dad merely gave me a blank look, and with everyone in the barbershop about to witness firsthand what he was truly made of, he said, "I'm not paying you anything for just getting your hair cut. What made you think I'd do that?"

Just like that, my father lost my trust. I ran out the door and down the street. He let me go for about two miles, allowing me to almost run home before he pulled up beside me and ordered, "Get in the car—now!"

I sat there fuming for a moment and then said, "You told me you'd give me five dollars for getting my haircut. You know you said it."

His response was short and to the point. "I don't care what I said. You're not some long-hair hippy, understand?" Indeed, I did. He was a man who no longer could be trusted.

Later that week, he and my mother got into a huge argument about how that Beatles poster was the source of my rebellion—whatever mild rebellion it was. And, in a final act of trying to turn back the clock, Dad ripped our poster off the wall, tearing it to pieces in front of us, telling us we should not look up to such degenerates.

Understanding the charity of Rockefeller's cloister stands in startling contrast to what was passed on to me by my father, a man who believed in nothing—no afterlife, not even a promise made to an eleven-year-old boy. Perhaps not such a strange memory for me to have called up while surrounded by hundreds of pieces of art that were inspired by faith.

The simplicity of The Cloisters transported me back to a medieval time, where protective stone walls deadened intrusive noise, reflected light into dark places, and that day the place offered me a hidden sanctuary. There, rays of afternoon light entered through unglazed gothic windows and diffused onto stone arches, columns, and walls. Streams of light and dust settled on Gothic artifacts, each placed opposite stone openings. There was a golden light present in the largest domed chapel, where Christ hung on the cross, a wooden statue meant to remind its viewers of His suffering.

The gardens were medieval too, simple plantings of rose or herbs within columned atriums, accompanied by the rhythm of flowing water. Each garden depicted an ordered setting where monks could have meditated. Mild breezes whispered off the river, cooling the heat of day and making the city seem much further away than it really was. The mind-numbing noise of modern man was dulled.

Departing this sanctuary, I was directed down a cold, dark hallway and out onto a cobblestone street, where a uniformed guard nodded as a car pulled up, and it and its driver whisked me forward in time.

11 Congaree National Park, South Carolina

July 28, 2007

Anna was annoyed about what she called my impulsive behavior to see "yet another" national park. I had a hunch from the start she intended to make this excursion a living hell for me, and she did just that. She felt forced to make this trip and was sick of my demands to see national parks. She told me I was obsessed with these trips and made the arrangements without consulting her, and she was right. Deep down it was bitter and sweet. Anna was not enthusiastic about the task which I'd undertaken, and I'd failed in communicating my reasons and zeal to her.

Despite my desire to help Olivia get another stamp for her national park book, the kids were siding with Anna's misery—each made an appeal to stay home to be with friends. But, somehow, cooperation cropped up as the kids piled into the car, reducing the friction. I turned over the engine, pulled out to wait for Anna in the driveway. Time passed. I honked the horn, which further exasperated the crew. The dog moved about the front seat, watching for Anna, nervous as though we would leave her behind this time, a feeling he knew too well—he usually watched us drive off from the front windows. Olivia yelled, "Stop honking the horn." Finally, Anna came out, and so with everyone in the car, we got a move on. Even Oliver, who just wanted to go wherever we went, couldn't get settled. His panting nervousness seemed more intense than usual. We drove without speaking, northeast to Columbia, South Carolina, moving along at a good clip.

We arrived at 5:30 that evening, and even I was feeling unwelcomed by South Carolina—the humidity was overpowering; it was the type of heat that turns faces red, causes tempers to flare, and melts all desire to move around.

I checked into the Marriott while the kids concealed Oliver in some sort of tote bag, smuggling him past the front desk into the elevator and up ten floors, letting him out to run down the hallway. Once in our rooms, Oliver ran straight to a window, which was too high for him to see out of. He jumped up, slammed into the glass and bounced off in a whimper. Though he did this only once, we couldn't help but stare at him. That was our chance at humor, voiding the honking, the silence of the drive, humidity's misery, the act of smuggling the dog, and transforming our rough start into one happy misadventure. All seemed forgotten in that moment, but that didn't last.

Sofia ran over to him. "Oliver, are you all right, boy?" He looked dazed and confused.

He knew he'd done something stupid—his tail still and between his legs as he looked at each of us with his cheerless black eyes.

Wanting to see some of Columbia, we smuggled Oliver out and walked maybe five blocks, sweating in no time, and entered the first sidewalk café we came upon. We found an outdoor table, fans spinning above, under which Oliver sat contentedly. But our iced Cokes and teas did little to cool our irritable moods. And to make matters worse, the waiter spilled a beer down Olivia's shirt and shorts. We cut out fast—retreated to our air-conditioned rooms.

As the evening heat settled, I convinced Anna to take a walk, thinking I could soften her up a bit. This was a college town, University of South Carolina, there must be a party somewhere, I thought. As we walked along, much to my amazement, we found a British high school orchestra performing outside in a museum's courtyard. Anna wanted nothing to do with me or the British. My annoying insistence on finding her a seat, coupled with my lame attempts to dull her anger were huge mistakes. I should have just let her stew, but I only know that in looking back. At the time, how could I have known? She'd had it with me, the music, and what she believed was an unnecessary trip—a waste of time and money.

To show her displeasure, she grimaced with that look I always know means I'm in the shit house. She always looks away after she gives that look, but this time, she got up during the concert and stormed off, leaving me there to look the fool. Eyes fell on me from all sides. I can only imagine what the concert-goers must have thought. I looked at some of them, swallowed my humility and got up to chase her, hoping the orchestra didn't stop and then start playing her declaration of war.

I watched Anna leave at a pace, which didn't allow me or, for that matter a sprinter, to catch her. She moved quickly to open a door, stood in the art museum's lobby, frowning, just waiting for me to pay her admission fee. Once the wallet appeared, she moved rapidly away to let them all know she was pissed and that I was an ass. We checked out the art separately. I tried to look interested in it all, but truthfully, I just wanted to smooth things over and get on with the trip. It wasn't a good scene at all. She was pissed because I forced her to swallow one more thing. I did not ask, but told her and without a second thought. She'd felt like I was treating her like some possession, like that jacket you take from the hanger when you need it. I just failed, wanting to have good times, which nagged at me too.

Anna wanted to eat, so we found a good restaurant on the strip, got us a table, and we ordered beers. We made small talk over fish, but there would be no dessert, no make-up sex—

each of us just wanted the evening to end, and sleep could not come soon enough. Back at the hotel in separate beds, she called over to Oliver to make sure he slept with her, a last message to me that I was not even inside the dog house that day.

I had hopes for the next day and thought we could salvage something from the trip. Just outside the town was Congaree National Park—a floodplain forest with boardwalk trails, a visitors center, and both fishing and canoeing. I had arranged for a ranger-guided canoe trip on the Cedar Creek.

We drove that morning to a marsh-covered access point and unloaded our canoes. We split into three rowing teams and boarded: Adam and Sofia in one; Anna, Olivia, and Oliver in another, and Hanna and me in the last canoe. It was our first time in canoes, and following the evening of instability, it was evidently only appropriate to continue in this fashion, only now on water. Collective amnesia must have set in, however, since once we were paddling, the mood changed to one of adventure and all was forgiven.

The creek meandered through forest wetlands, and the treetops provided a canopy from the sun's intense heat. The trees were of the marsh variety with wide, funnel-shaped bases narrowing to a single main trunk. Packed into the wetland ecosystem, bald cypress roots reached out like octopus tentacles, securing their trunks in the muddy creek bottom. Water tupelo, American elms, and oaks huddled together to form a dense forest that was covered in gray sea grass, which hung without motion, forming overgrown moss tunnels that snaked through creek offshoots.

A brown snake—some sort of moccasin was sunning itself on a nearby branch; turtles slipped from rocks when they heard our paddles on the water, and birds chattered overhead. The creek was low, which tested our limited skills to maneuver the canoes over fallen, water-logged trees resting just below the surface. We soon landed on a muddy shore at a cove, and as Anna stepped from the canoe, her unbalanced gait landed her in murky water. "Whoops, completely soaked!" She just laughed. I could see her sense of humor coming back—perhaps just a tickle of softening had begun during our float.

On our return trip, Oliver joined my boat, manning the bow with careful observation of not only his family, but also the sounds and movements of the impressive ecosystem surrounding us.

To say our three-day excursion to Congaree National Park wasn't brimming with family harmony would be an understatement, since I was apparently just shoving national parks up everyone's ass. I thought I was putting together one more getaway, but as life dictates, my plan backfired that time.

12 Fathers and Sons

Looking back to when Mom and Dad were still married, when we were family, my pre-teen years seemed normal enough, if not mundane. There was orderliness, sameness. I can't say if they were boring years because I know no better.

My father liked to watch the six o'clock news, while Mom, draped in an apron, completed her bon vivant meals. Around six-thirty, she'd shout, "Dinner," then repeat it. We sat, bowed our heads and hushed. Dad said the same blessing as if it was history. The food was passed with that sameness, and then, like everything else that's had its time, dinner rushed forward. Dad was an extremely quick eater. Mom would ring his bell each night with, "You're not in a horse race, Paul," followed by, "Kids, take three bites of everything." She would not allow anyone to leave the table until the three-bite rule was enforced and all forks lay at rest. After dinner, James and I cleared the table, washed dishes. Lynn, escaped to the bathroom; she was only five, so she deserved this chore amnesty.

When that was over, we gathered in the living room to watch our new color TV. Around eight-thirty we were shuffled off to bed, giving Mom and Dad a break to watch the evening news, Johnny Carson, their shows. It couldn't have been that rewarding. There was only a hand-full channels, and you had to get up to turn the dial, rotate the antenna with another compass-like device until a picture appeared without bars running through the image like some 8mm film. No channel surfing back then. It was too complicated. First you'd find the TV Guide, suggest a program, debate its content and hope the weather would not affect the picture. But then again, that was all that they knew—all any of us knew. Despite the dinner blessing, prayer was never a part of it, though. Dad did scream "goddamnit" a lot, at the TV, but I don't think He ever showed up to help with that. Sundays were different because we watched *The Wonderful World of Disney* together.

The routine never changed, never veered—week after monotonous week.

James and I played baseball during the season. Dad took us to tryouts, practices, and games on Saturdays. Win or lose, we were treated to candy. Sometimes we even dined at a fast-food joint, always Jack-in-the-Box. And with these acts of baseball and fast food, Dad stretched out our memory of his fatherhood, though he never really seemed engaged, but more as though acting like he thought a father should.

Dad also liked taking us to the parks, where we played on jungle-gyms or some other merry-go-round or see-saw contraption. It was his impulse that got us out of the house, and it always seemed like the thing to do, a trait passed on, I guess. But Dad wasn't a big fan of sand and beach. I don't know why, he just could not overlook his objections to the party on the beach, so we really never went—beach party or not, though we lived in San Diego.

Instead, he thought to provide our fun through his connections at work. Dad had access to sailboats, which became his private research project. This was terrifying because he didn't know how to sail. Once he sailed into a restricted Navy submarine zone where sailors screamed and waved their guns.

He almost sank the boat in that panic. Then there was the time when he left the bay just the once, and the ocean winds took the little boat to a point where waters rushed into the stern. There were also the feared, unannounced "come-abouts" that could send you flying if the boom caught you.

We started making these trips when Mom started her weekend binges, just after her brother, our Uncle David, passed. David served in the Navy during Vietnam. He came to live with us for awhile after his tour. Once, he fell asleep in the living room with a lit cigarette that burned a hole in Mom's new couch. He left for home in Chicago shortly after that. Dad parroted over and over about how he'd burn the house down and kill us all.

I'm not sure what the greater danger was back then. The sailing had its risks of drowning, and maybe if we hadn't made our weekend excursions which took us away from Mom, she might not have been so easily able to drown in her drinks. Our guilt was sort of an anti-bargain because Dad came with fewer obligations. So Dad took the deal, gathered us and carted us off to the park or to another terrifying test of his sailing skills. He meant well. We knew it was his way of concealing Mom's addiction to booze and pills, a scene which we would find on each homecoming.

Mother's meals stopped too. They were replaced with TV dinners and TV trays, which cut down on the bullshit chores. Lynn didn't have to go to the bathroom as much either.

Then there were the bridge nights when we were sent to our rooms. Everyone had the presence of mind to know that drinks, cards, cigarette smoke and adult conversation were not to be interrupted by children, but we could still hear the sounds of bridge-card gossip.

One particular night, the cards, ashtrays and bottles were not set out, and there was tension. We could all tell. After the guests arrived, we heard the crashing of chairs, screams and the rumble of fighting. We ran down the hall to find Dad and Tom Tatom caught up in a brawl, like two rams exchanging blows. We were rooting for Dad—first fist fight we'd ever seen. Dad screamed, "Never contact her again, asshole," which was strange since they'd been friends with the Tatom family for years. I suspected after the "asshole" comment they were fighting because Mother must have been putting out while Dad worked nights or on those weekend bridge trips she would take with other men. It was ordinary, how she planned those trips. We all knew the details; she was a grand master or something, needed certain bridge partners, and Dad was no good at it, so when the men picked her up and put the suitcase in the trunk, Dad took us to the park. I guess it was some form of denial, or was just accepted as part of the times. But not that evening. The fight marked my father's retreat from the family, and none of us knew the better.

That night sitting in bed, they screamed at each other, the walls just closed in. I was scared shitless that they would be beating each other next. It was just a matter of time. Had our luck run out that night, and to a man that played cards? There was a lot I wanted ask in the midst of all the riot—"Are you two getting divorced?" "Are we going to move?" I barricaded my head and my anxiety under pillows to squelch the yelling.

Looking back, it's clear to me my family had hit the point of no return, and in that moment, though we didn't know, I was, we all were, watching our own family's destruction. Each situation takes a turn, a direction, leading to the next development. The developments can bring both promise and destruction, and they still do—always looking back in order to look ahead.

When I think about it, Uncle David's death, like that fight between Mom's lover and Dad, was also one of those tipping points. But this tipping point was earlier and more insidious. Mom's brother hanged himself in their mother's basement. I imagine that he probably left a note, but my grandmother kept that and whatever secrets it contained. David's death allowed Mom's self-pity and denial to grow, and everyone around her permitted her to wallow in it. This wasn't David's tragedy, it was her tragedy.

So, Mom married Tom Tatom several years after her divorce. He was the next source of income, and it was convenient. He couldn't replace Dad, and we made it miserable for him. We dealt out shame, our own self-pity, our own misfortunes. It was the game of fish that boiled over, burning dear Tom. Their marriage was short, and I'm sure we were a disappointment to her. But she should have known this was simply the next step in her family fiasco.

Through all that, I'd think back to those days when we had some semblance of unity. Like the fact that every year the family made the drive from San Diego to Anaheim for a day at Disneyland. Again, it was always carried out by the numbers. It was a routine—one I grew to miss. We'd stop at the same restaurant, just off the freeway. My order never changed: A grilled-cheese sandwich, fries, and chocolate malt, topped with whipped cream stained red where a Maraschino cherry sat, which I believed were the only type of cherries in existence, and they were in every restaurant I ate at and refrigerator I opened.

Other than Disneyland, there were a couple of other family trips when I was very young, when Uncle David was still alive, when my mother didn't drink. We drove to Chicago once to visit our grandparents and my mother's siblings, David and Susan. Uncle David was the hippest; he listened to the cool music, had a convertible, green BMW and would take us to the Navy base. He had been an officer, crew-cut black hair covered by a plain, black visor where an eagle shield sat on crossed anchors above. He wore a pressed navy uniform with colored bars over his heart. He seemed so proud wearing that hat and suit, telling us about Vietnam, which seemed irrational to me given all the killing on the TV. When he wasn't wearing it, it hung on the outside of the closet door, always visible. The Navy base was fenced in, made it seem cloak-and-dagger, with guards who asked for passes, and once in, past the rows of barracks, was a warehouse where you could buy things cheap. Rows of provisions, cigarettes and booze, which is what Uncle David bought since it was a shore-leave of sorts.

The one real highlight of my youth was a trip to Yosemite. To this day I can close my eyes and travel back to that place. I see the trees, smell the air, and feel the terrain beneath my feet.

Yosemite was where we camped along a meandering river that was tucked inside the park's spectacular carved granite valley and which was fed by the mighty Yosemite Falls. The river's beach stones were ground granite, colors of all types and a little rough on the bare feet. Half Dome was in sight through the trees, and at night, the rangers dropped burning coals from a granite pike, calling the tradition the "Fire Fall," an act which they don't do anymore, burned up some chipmunks and several bunnies in the process, I guess? We camped in this concrete bunker, complete with beds and a small table where we ate. Meals were simple, cooked on a fire or on a metal grill. We were all in and together that week. There were smiles and laughter and bears too—we were family, like all the other families who had come in their cars with different colored license plates that we counted each morning on our way to the bathrooms to shower. To my young mind, this was an exotic adventure—and looking back, it was the best time our family ever had together, and it left a mark. It made a normal, happy family life seem possible.

But there was only one vacation such as this. And for the longest time, it remained a lone memory until those trips Anna and I took with our kids to those places that I so wanted in my past and needed to be in their memories.

Before Adam, Hanna, Olivia and Sofia arrived, Anna and I traveled a bit, had sex everywhere, and on one of our trips, conceived Adam in Stockholm, in the Grand Hotel. (I know this as fact because Anna can recall each moment of conception for our four children: Hanna was San Diego; Olivia was Alpharetta, and Sofia was Paris). Adam was born in San Diego and weighed in at close to ten pounds.

We took him home and were introduced to the diapers, bottles, and strollers that were built to crash test specs like some Ferrari. Adam slept in our bed, nestled between us, for over a year. We took him everywhere and truly believed our son was some sort of celebrity. When we were out, we overheard things, thought everyone was admiring our boy. First-time parent pride is blinding, but vanishes after the second child arrives when you realize it is an invented arrogance.

I carried Adam with me in a backpack though the desert, along the California coast, and through Yosemite a couple of times. He sat in Anna's lap on the airplane en route to his baptism in Sweden, which was a hell of a flight. It was his first time on a plane, and it scared the shit out of him.

I was overjoyed being a father. It gave me purpose. My thoughts often drifted to the future we'd have together—an eternity of wondrous moments, measured out in days and years—fantasizing about what sports Adam would play in high school and college, and even daydreamed that we'd even go into business together—a father and son operation. I wanted to do all the things my father never offered. It was subconsciously my way to over-correct because I'd never settled up with my dad.

To me, fatherhood was priceless—not up for sale, a bond that'd only grow. It was palpable each time Adam and I made eye contact, how his baby head turned to greet me every time I entered a room, or whenever he heard my voice. For the most part it remained that way. I could go downstairs to surprise him in his room playing video games, those eyes were there, so pure and easy to look at.

We heard Adam's first word: "Mama," watched him crawl like an ant on the carpet in our new home in San Diego. Then, he took his first steps, and soon he was riding his bicycle on the grass in our backyard, and it didn't feel like much later that he fell in love with a girl who would make sure he'd play her straight.

I always wished I could slow it down, press pause or rewind, stop to take it all in, stay in the moment, find a still point. Anna and I didn't want to miss a thing. Adam was growing fast, and it was impossible to record it all, which we could've done a better job of.

There are pictures of him playing baseball at age eight, something that ended as a one-season fling because we discovered tennis. And off we went, at least two or three times each week, to our subdivision's courts. I couldn't wait to make it home from work. We were together at least an hour across the net, and then we'd jump in the pool to cool off.

And Oliver, our faithful third—always there with us—we were, after all, the three boys of the house. Oliver was castrated, though not sure he knew it. We were inseparable, given the fact we could be next, but in some other, more subtle way.

Adam started tennis lessons when he was ten. I sat and watched virtually every ball he hit or missed for the next ten years. He got to the point, which we all knew would come, when he finally beat me. What a joy to experience such a loss. Our weekends were spent traveling to tournaments. Hanna soon joined us. When she was about twelve and had grown into a very good player herself, she could win just on stubborn. And so it went on for more than three years like that, the three of us sort of went rogue.

I knew tennis would be one of our lifelong bonds; we'd play together for the rest of our lives. I'd close my eyes and do something almost any parent does, imagine their child in the future. I saw Adam teaching his own children the game's intricacies, just as I had taught them to him.

Our family took tennis vacations where we played on grass and clay courts. And by doing so, built memories for all of us, I'd hoped. Adam's progression seemed without limits; in due time he and Hanna were state-ranked, something more important to me than to them. Nonetheless, the two were proud to see their names and ranking listed online. I loved to pull that website up at work, just to make sure they were there.

Yes, I knew Adam would always be there—even after he married and had his own children because my son would admire and trust his father.

Then high school began, and for the first time in his life, Adam seemed lost. He was good-looking beyond ordinary, had friends, but the pressures to fit in, to succeed, and to know his direction were on his mind. For a parent, this agony is something to endure in silence, which is nearly impossible, when they come to you with their plans, which are never complete and are articulated with such twists and turns of direction, it amuses, then becomes loads of fun just to listen to. These conversations became peaceful for me, and they were something to wait for.

Sure enough, Adam's struggles to find a direction for his adult life ceased during his sophomore year. He discovered his passion when he built his own computer. Such was his excitement that he declared: "Dad, I'm going to work at Intel after I get my PhD in computer engineering." And, by the grace of love, I knew then for sure that I'd do everything I could to help him achieve this goal.

Adam had faith very young, which drove his beliefs, and he came to me when he needed to be reassured, which I hope I did for him. I could, at that point, tell him he was bright, smart and that he was on the right path in his life. For a kid in high school to ask if there was a heaven threw Anna and me back. Then, one afternoon coming home from tennis, he told me his Jesus story, and it was a story about loving others deeply, especially this one girl, Stephanie.

In his junior year, he fell in love with Stephanie—his first real girlfriend. That put me on the sideline, an uncomfortable place for any parent, as I watched my son's love magnify—I saw his happiness, his loving compassion, all so touching when seeing first love again. Love's impulse called Adam to do crazy things to win Stephanie's heart, which he did in words and in unearthing four-leaf clovers, and putting on a suit and tie for special dates. I got to tie that tie for him.

Stephanie was the perfect companion for Adam. And even though I was replaced, we still talked, father-to-son, about her and how she'd be the first forever, how not to neglect her needs, not so much tennis anymore. We talked about future inventions and the hurt when something goes wrong in a relationship. He listened to me, but though he had it down, all under control, I recognized that boy inside there, knew him well as a version of my younger self.

I knew he and Stephanie were having sex in the basement, never confronted them, though I did go down once and made lots of noise clanking around as if I was deconstructing the basement, then I heard the door slam, a ten-second escape for Stephanie. Adam sat there with a frantic look on his face, amazed he wasn't caught naked.

Adam had grown up, our conversations told me this. His well-formed thoughts and opinions showed his deeply established independence and self-esteem. His heart was, indeed, in the right place. He was always kind and sympathetic to others.

Once, Adam asked his mother and me if one of his friends, Nick, could live with us for a while. Nick had been a product of a divorce, an alchoholic father, and he was about to fail a class that he needed to graduate. We did it for Adam. The kid moved back home with his father in about three weeks, guess he couldn't stand my writing lessons and the rules that I forced on him in those first days in the house.

Granted, we did have our problems, and Nick's moving in was not a good call. I was overbearing, trying to make Adam a tennis star, which he only wanted to do for me. I screamed and yelled about grades, a Mohawk haircut, and other shit that simply didn't matter in the final shakedown. I was an idiot, just like my father, but I hope to a lesser extent. Looking back, I tried to do just the opposite of what my dad did. The Mohawk haircut must have triggered something, but years later Anna and I would wear Adam's Mohawk with pride.

I did what I could to ensure our father-son relationship

and forced it when I thought I needed to. I deeply needed to prove our relationship not only to him, but to myself.

Adam as a teenager was slim, yet muscular, almost six-feet tall. His blue eyes had an intensity when he looked at you. It was not a stare, but a direct connection—the kind that engendered trust. He was constantly smiling. His lips curved to form small dimples on rosy cheeks, which caused his eyes to squint and smile too. His nose, a perfect button, was still wholly masculine. His brown, curly hair was always a little messy—kind of like mine, actually. He was Mr. Happy.

As a little boy he experienced his first successful fishing expedition. The joy of catching and landing a trout quickly disappeared when, holding the fish in his hands, he believed the fish was dead. His eyes looked so sad. But when the trout wiggled, Adam laughed—not overjoyed about his angling prowess, but simply thrilled he had not marred the universe. I can recall Adam's smile, have a picture of it, as he returned that trout to the river.

Then, years later, he was with his younger cousin, Roger, as they stood together on the shores of La Jolla cove, Adam was wearing his shirt that read, "Swedes are björn to rock!" Adam guided Roger along that day. When Adam's smile broke to joy, it was a pure pleasure, and he spread his grin as if the sun was shining on both their faces.

And on one of Hanna's birthdays, Adam took his time, made her a big birthday card. On it he placed a color picture of Hanna as a small child, standing nude complete with white wings—his vision of her as a little angel. Hanna keeps the card by her bedside now.

Olivia would go to Adam's room and listen to his music. If she tried to leave, he wouldn't let her go, "Don't leave, stay some more," which she did often. Little Sofia, Adam's baby sister, looked to him for sisterly assurances whenever Hanna and Olivia went on the attack. And he defended her.

And then Adam's grin was ever-present when he was in the company of Stephanie, his true love. To witness his eyes bonding with hers, then watching them hug; to see their joy and hear their laughter was priceless.

For reasons I can't understand, my dad seldom came to see either me or his grandchildren and remained stingy with his love, always attaching money to it. Over the past ten years, he visited us only two or three times, always in the company of Judy, his insane and selfish-bitch third wife. Judy never allowed my father much peace, and she was always trying to draw attention to herself with her screeching voice and bizarre behavior. Once she shrieked so loud in a restaurant that the place went silent, all because the trout she ordered still had its head attached.

Adam came with me when I visited my father, who was dying cancer's slow death. It was that one last hope. His body was like broken twigs. Judy, his cuckoo bird, had played nurse forty years ago as a sort of career and for my father's benefit or otherwise, and she was glad to revive her role as such. Her medications were as mad-capped as shock treatments and open radiation tubes. We were standing outside the wooded gate and fence that surrounded my father's house, which she had dead-bolted shut. She refused to let us in, while inside she was conducting unscheduled feedings of crushed morphine, telling him it was an old man's best friend. She spooned the dust to his chapped tongue. She wouldn't allow hospice care, couldn't justify the cost. Adam had to scale the wall and unlock the gate. He never really got to know his grandfather. This trip was the memory that stood out for him.

Adam saw first-hand just how selfish family can be. What upset me was that my father not only never took the time to get to know Adam nor any of his own eight living grandchildren, but sometimes seemed like he was actally running away from them. Adam felt sorry for my dad, and he was tender with this dying man. We spent several days with Dad, mostly sitting around the house. Once we went and got donuts, which Dad loved to eat. We talked some, and Dad insisted that Adam read to him, which he did, maybe the one thing Dad would remember about Adam. Then, there were the limits Judy put on everything, making sure Adam and I didn't make any lasting impressions. She needed his attention in the end as she tried to change his will to her benefit. Adam saw all this and knew his grandfather had allowed one of life's gifts to slip through—that relationship between father and son.

Adam could feel the anxiety between his grandfather and me, and as he stared at me on the plane ride back home, he told me how sorry he felt about the whole thing. I told him it was alright, been that way too long to remember, and that I had him and his sisters now. That was the last time I saw my father alive. We said our goodbyes, then I told him we had to go. I got my crying done without crying for him. I saved those tears and only rubbed my eyes shut.

13 Pass Christian, Mississippi

August 8, 2007

Anna and I met Tim and Megan Moran in New York City in 1991. We had Adam and Hanna, and they had two kids too. We lived in the same high-rise on Roosevelt Island, rode the same elevators together for a year and a half. Their son, Tyler, had recovered from leukemia, and they had a little girl Emma; our four kids were all about the same age. We watched them grow, run down hallways in costumes on Halloween, chase birds on the park grass, bundled them in the New York winters, and we've been friends ever since. So Anna and I always looked forward to any excursion with them. Even though Tim and Megan moved to Washington D.C., we often met in the Mississippi Delta.

Tim and Megan are abundantly blessed and bought a house in Pass Christian, but just a couple of weeks after they closed the deal, Katrina drowned the house and took the entire town with it. They're not ones who give up, so Tim began the rebuilding process, and they continued to have children.

There in Mississippi's awe-inspiring Delta, the summer was cooled by breezes, which settled the heat of the long days. It was always good to visit our friends there. I remember sitting out, cooling myself on the veranda, the stillness sometimes broken by small fish leaping at bugs at rest on the bog's placid evening skin. The water was a deep green, upon which were cast the reflections and shadows of the trees that had happened to survive the Gulf storms. And as the sun set, the day gently dissipated, and all human sound was lost to crickets; the evening sky turned dark. And as the wind died away, all of us drifted off to sleep.

The new day always arrived quickly there, always putting us that much closer to the trek back home. The early morning's calm was thwarted by the padding of bare feet on wood floors and stairs. Megan was usually the first to rise, if only to stay one step ahead of the chaos. I remember her baby cuddled in her arms as she greeted Tim, who was the last to leave the comfort of bed. He jokingly surveyed the house, just to make sure it was still standing. Granted, the Moran homestead was not known for extended periods of stillness. They have many children of their own, and add Anna, Adam, Olivia, Hanna, Sofia, Oliver, and me to the mix, and you have...well, let's just say we pushed the envelope on the definition of household.

Card games were ongoing—Megan loved spades. There were children in the pool, waters always too warm to really cool you down. Tommy had fishing poles baited and cast. A dog sat next to him staring at the waters. Tim fueled the boats. Adam and Tyler rode the jet skis, and then there was the constant sound of a ping pong ball being slapped about in the open garage as I wrote.

On this particular morning, the Delta tide was high, and schools of fish rippled the surface en route to nowhere in particular. A breeze kicked up, then withered. Soon, the deeply humid heat settled in, everyone adjusting as cool bayou waters called us. Hours passed. Gray clouds accumulated, which cooled the air, leaving raindrops. Heaven's zenith arrived late. The crimson sky and purple clouds were strung along the horizon as their color dangled silently from limbs. The silver patches burned up the remaining light as its white sheets hung on until dusted into darkness.

There weren't grand waterfalls, redwoods, or astonishing architecture, but there was this drooping charm like the seagrass draping the trees.

It was Tim Moran's fortieth birthday, our friend of sixteen years; our gift to him was a facial and a fountain pen, which he will never use, since he writes with only pencils. The look Tim's youngest son, Tommy, gave him was priceless, as he thought of his father doing this feminine thing, also thinking to him-self, "Men should not get facials from other men" (meaning me). Tim enjoyed this curious attention, as the other children learned about that good thing that can bring unannounced joy and laughter, then Tim let all his children cut his hair.

14 Bluffs Lodge, North Carolina

October 6, 2007

School was going well for the kids. Adam built his own computer, and our time together seemed even more imperative to me than ever. They were growing fast. It had been two months since our last road trip to the Delta. My urgencies were truly inexplicable. There was something about the discoveries we made as a family that drove my desire to share the world right then and there with Anna and the kids. We had been to this lodge before, sitting in chairs outside the rooms, on the wooden second floor balcony which overlooked nothing but deep nature—the kind that can swallow you or that you could find yourself in. We looked forward to our return, where we could disappear down some trail, lose ourselves in wilderness talking about previous trips or simply the day or hour before, or the streaks in the granite in the mountain. We drove, doing what it seemed we must do, and went down the paths that just went on turning.

We arrived at the Blue Ridge Mountains very late after a long, nighttime journey, which was often the case when we left for trips after I got in from work. Anna picked up the kids from three different schools, and we met back at the house and off we drove. Two room keys had been left in the unlocked office, no check-in required. Anna, Olivia, and Hanna piled into one room with two double beds, while Adam, Sofia, and I settled into the room next door.

Adam and Sofia climbed straight into their bed, and then it began—the endless conversations and laughter, which was only one of the reasons we traveled like that. I loved to hear everyone laughing and carrying on about this and that.

"You should never listen to Mom's directions," Adam said.

89

"She took us eighteen miles off course at one in the morning."

As much as it would pain me later to side against Anna, I laughed and said, "I don't know why I did it, either. Next time I'll just go in the opposite direction."

We shared laughter's many rhythms—tonight's were mostly episodes of delirium.

Then, from out of nowhere, Sofia asked, "Do they have blueberry pancakes? I forgot. I guess I can't have the bacon. I love cows."

"What do cows have to do with bacon?" said Adam.

Sofia soon discovered that bacon did not come from cows, which carried the discussion to the differences between pigs and hogs.

"You know pigs and hogs are the same thing, and you owe me twenty bucks on that bet we had on our last trip," Sofia added. "Do you got the money?"

"Yeah, Dad, you need to pay her," Adam responded, supporting his sister's pig-hog theory. After all, he knew his backing would ensure her support in the future. He knew how to play this game.

Sofia's razor-sharp mind at ten was never at rest. In the blink of an eye, she could change the subject. "Can I have a baby pig for a pet?"

Knowing this was a one-time request, I countered, "Let me think about that one."

And so went our winding-down session, which, more often than not, in those late hours bordered on the ridiculous. Nonetheless, we were never at a loss for words—or laughter.

Bluffs Lodge was part of a small group of lodges in the national park system, most of which were usually old, well-built, and situated in the most beautiful parts of the country. I got these facts from the book *National Park Lodges*, which gives details about rooms, rates, food, seasons, as well as provides maps of the area and pencil illustrations of the establishments.

I only wished I could take the whole family to all of them as I checked off the ones we'd been to.

In the center of Bluff Lodge was a grand outdoor veranda, which overlooked the eroded hills and green meadows of the Appalachian Mountains. This two-story granite terrace was supported by a massive stone wall, and on each side were grand staircases descending to the meadow below. The heart of this gathering place was an enormous stone fireplace, which blazed late into the night. Adam took it upon himself to keep the fires stoked each night, adding one or two logs as guests idled away the evening in fifties-style chairs, getting to know each other while roasting marshmallows and sipping drinks.

The kids studied, as best they could, the design, layout, and craftsmanship of these spectacular lodges that were situated to invite the rustic-living types. We met old timers who'd strike up conversations as we, too, became lodge-seekers.

One evening there was a man and his wife, both of whom couldn't take their eyes off Adam and me, and they finally asked, "Were you here last year? We remember you two from last fall."

"Yes," I told them. "We were here last year, heard about this place in a newspaper." They told us that they'd been coming to this lodge for years, and I recalled how Adam and I had been sitting in those same seats the year before at this very time, doing the very same thing around this fireplace. Adam got up put another log on the fire and asked if they would like a marshmallow, while with his free hand, he staked two on the straightened wire hanger. They couldn't resist.

Mornings, the veranda's stone parapet became a focal point. It was here that guests congregated to enjoy the view, read or just relax. In the field below, a stacked-wood fence ran along and around a small hill, giving an aged border to green pastures. In the distance, the brow-line of a Manzanita was perfectly scenic with black-and-white Holstein cows grazing in a barbed wire fence that ran along, climbing and dipping with the slope of the hills.

It was early fall when we were there, and the mountain air was cool with a slight breeze, not yet full chill, the leaves were just turning. Across the bluff to the west, the hillside was resplendent with evergreens, Virginia pines, white pines, oaks, hemlock, spruce, and firs. Nearby, were large oaks with their Christmas-tree-shaped leaves fluttering. Depending on the time of day and the slant of the sun, shades of green, reddish-brown, bright yellow, and burned-red patches harmonized in the view.

Olivia and Sofia pulled a red wagon along the balcony, those superior fall colors as their backdrop. They had eleven freshly picked leaves: one green, another red-tipped, beside which rested a light-green, two black-spotted, another yellow, one deep red, another reddish-yellow, two dark brown, and one a deeper shade of brown. The girls arranged each leaf side-by-side, a progression of fall color.

Soon Hanna was screaming down a hill in the wagon, Adam running behind, while Anna arrived with two more leaves to add to the collection, plus the following written words in black ink on two scraps of paper:

> The faded leaf lay fallen to the ground, waiting to fulfill its purpose. Not long ago it had soared high above the rocky fields that lay below. Proudly waving its glory in the wind, it sang tribute to its creator. With all its might, it served its host until one day the fall wind took hold, and with a last exuberant dance, it sailed to the ground to find its destiny, its place of rest.

But it was the sunset that pampered the eye; the bright rays dropped a veil on the treetops—an orange glow above and between the branches that would face fall's moonrise.

There was no ignoring nature there.

That was our fourth family trip to Bluffs Lodge. It's relaxing nature and beauty got better each time. There was an old, rustic restaurant within walking distance, and the fried chicken, biscuits, and pleasant manners were from another era. Anna and I hoped that and wondered if someday our children would bring their children here and read these words to them.

15 San Diego's Cabrillo National Monument

October 13, 2007

From Bluffs Lodge to the Atlanta airport, only a week had passed. Olivia was twelve going on teenager and was excited to take off from school and go on her first business trip with me. She packed as if she were heading up the meetings herself: Business suits of sorts. It was a joy to take her along, and my first priority was making sure we found lots of time to be just father and daughter.

Anna and I had left San Diego sixteen years ago with Adam and Hanna and moved to New York City in 1991, then south to Alpharetta, Georgia in 1993. Olivia joined us about a year after that. For me, going back to San Diego can be bittersweet, since my mother and father began their implosion there forty-nine years ago. However, Olivia could take the sting off most anything.

The flight over I thought back to when I was about six, and my parents decided to have me baptized. This was my first dose of religion, and it was a frightening experience. I don't remember the name of the church, but it was on a street corner in downtown San Diego. I do remember my baptism though.

I was clueless as to the events that were about to unfold that morning. My mother told me if I didn't get baptized, I could go to hell. That Sunday I was taken up to the altar—it felt like a sacrifice. Standing with just the pastor in front of the congregation, I was alone. He said some words, then anointed my head with the ritual water and spoke to the crowd and me: "I would like to introduce John Stephens. Please introduce yourself to everyone."

I turned my head to see hundreds of piercing eyes, fear flowed inside me. I felt so exposed, I cracked. I flew down from the altar, running past Mom and Dad, through the turning heads and burst through the church doors. In this profession of faith and the hymn of the parishioners' laughter came my father, for which I was grateful. Embarrassed as I was, I didn't want to be alone, and he made me feel love without judgment and without ever speaking a word. We left the church shortly after that and stopped going altogether. I wasn't sure exactly what their decision was based upon, but it felt like humiliation mixed with shame, probably from what I'd done.

It was a few years after the baptismal fiasco when we moved to the suburbs and joined the First Methodist Church in La Mesa, California. Mom would dress James and me in clip-on ties and patten leather shoes and pack us off to Sunday school rooms, where we suffered through the readings of Old Testament stories about Noah and a Red Sea parting. None of this seemed relevant to me. The teachers read the stories with such monotony that kids would fall asleep, and those of us who kept awake resided in hellish boredom. Relief only came each Sunday when they rang the church bells at noon at the end of the adult service. That's when we'd race from the room to the courtyard, where we'd join our parents for cookies, lemonade and coffee, then play with the other kids on the boulders out front.

But this was only a prelude to the really fun part. My father's next destination was just a short drive down Mount Helix to Anthony's Fish Grotto—a place I marveled at over and over again as a child. The Grotto had a big pond with waterfalls coming off the roof. Through the eyes of a child, it seemed as if ducks were everywhere, and we could feed them. We'd buy a cup of duck food for a nickel and have them eating out of our hands in no time. The ducks were quick. No matter how hard we tried, we never were able to pet them, only chase them around. And if we tried to reach out for one of the ducklings, mama and daddy duck would snap at us.

After feeding the ducks, we'd sit down to lunch. Mine was always the same—a tuna fish sandwich on toast, fries and a Shirley-Temple with one of those Maraschino cherries floating in the ice.

What I remember most, though, was fidgeting throughout the week, waiting for Sunday to arrive—the ride to church, the boring class, the cookies and the Grotto, wondering if this was going to be the week I'd finally catch and hold a duckling. But I had to get through the whole week first—the whole week, the class, the same stories—all for the payoff—the ducks. It was worth it. And the fact that I remember all that so well, only reaffirms that it was more worth it than I knew. I longed to feel secure in the knowledge that we'd always spend our Sundays in this fashion—shared meals, shared laughter, always as a family.

Whenever opportunity presents itself, I visit the Grotto. It's now part of my adult pilgrimage back West. Although the water is now surrounded by a chain-link fence, the ducks still roam. And they still avoid me in all my persistence at trying to pet them. I've outgrown tuna fish-on-toast with fries though. Little else has changed—including the feeling of peace the Grotto gives me.

I've taken Anna there many times. She likes this blue concoction served with a slice of pineapple skewered on a miniature blue marlin. She jokes, "I've saved all the blue marlins."

On this trip, I watched Olivia insert her nickel into the same machine that I inserted my nickels in as a boy, getting her cup of duck food. I told her how I used to feed the ducks, and how the chain link fence was not there back then, and show her where her mother and I sat when we dated. Olivia liked feeding the ducks—giggled as they skittered away from her outstretched hand.

After our Grotto visit and a drive by my old house to show Olivia where I grew up, Olivia and I resumed our journey and headed to visit my sister Lynn, Roger, her husband, and their son, Little Roger. We drove together along the West Coast Road, past the graves of soldiers buried in the Point Loma cemetery, where Roger's grandfather was buried, and we stopped to touch the tombstone, then continued on to Cabrillo National Monument. The salt air and west winds kept the dry scrub-brush surrounding the monument on the hill low, and the branches were well-weathered by the winds' constant bearing. We arrived atop a hill at a nautical point. Olivia took Little Roger's hand, and they ran to the top of the hill. To the west was the Pacific, and to the east was a deep-water bay. From that vantage point, we not only saw the rocky shorelines and coastal tidal pools, but heard the muffled sound of waves slamming the coastline.

I got Little Roger a national park passport book too. For the most part, the trip went well, and Olivia got her first West Coast stamp as did her cousin. For reasons I don't understand, Lynn's husband is a self-isolated man and actually reminds me of my father in a lot of ways. He does love my sister, but only his own family blood runs dear to him. Compassion seems beyond his grasp, or maybe that's the way he wishes to be perceived.

16 Thanksgiving

November 21, 2007

It always began with a kind invitation to share bounty with dear friends and family at Pass Christian. Then it escalated to our children talking about seeing what they call their "first cousins." And that's all true. Anna and I see our good friends Tim and Megan and their seven children as family—blood.

We departed late Tuesday, stayed at some roadside hotel and arrived Wednesday morning to a rush of children welcoming us. At the top of the stairs was Megan with her baby scooped into her arms. Babies never seemed to stop arriving for this woman, and we'd added six more folks to their table.

The main item up for discussion was "can we do something to help," and the menu—the size of the turkey, a ham or not, mashed potatoes, sweet potatoes, which vegetables—and, best of all, how we couldn't wait to inhale the aroma of Megan's apple and pumpkin pies. It was always this way, the meal's fine-tuning. Last-minute ingredients were needed as the recipes were reread, which caused frequent trips to the market—a market that should have already been closed for the holiday.

The first order of business on Thursday morning was always the bird, exhibited in the kitchen and admired by everyone. It was stuffed, seasoned, and prepared with Megan's usual care. Anna opened the oven door and helped Megan place the bird on the center rack. As expected, all the day's activities centered on the kitchen—preparing, nibbling, and anticipating the meal to come. Even Oliver sat under the table hoping something would drop to the floor.

The bird cooked slowly, as always. And as its fragrance permeated the house, our hunger pangs grew to a feverish pitch. Megan and Anna prepared plate after plate of food; the kitchen was bustling with activity—chopping, pots hissing beyond the boil, and the two chicks in aprons running back and forth. Something was missing for a recipe, and I was sent to the store with five kids to round out the list. They sent the kids with me, so I didn't screw up, and I'm sure it gave the girls a break back at the kitchen. The day passed slowly despite all the activity, like no other day of the year. Thanksgiving's clock was that most deliberate ticking of golden-brown perfection. It was unhurried precision, leisurely exactness, which awaited the cook's practiced eye and prompted the two most anticipated words: "It's ready."

The turkey was placed on the counter for all to see. The best knife had been sharpened, watched closely by Adam, who was to one day get the honor of carving the bird. We watched as the tender carvings were placed on the largest plate in the house. Small pieces were cut and tasted, as the smell of the dressing and gravy spread through the house. With all domestic disobediences and chaos that nearly a dozen hungry children can provide dissolved, we all brought the food to the table—and the meal began. Kids moved in and took their spots at the table, which was packed in like a rugby team around the ball.

There were nineteen at the table. The parents and grandparents took their seats, and all was ready for the big pig-out. But before we passed around the food, we paused for a moment of thanks, which Tim led. Our dinner was only interrupted by a Jack Russell that nudged me gently to remind me of his infinite loyalty.

17 Chicago, Illinois

December 15, 2007

It was our second Christmas trip to one of the great cities of the United States—a journey that would take us to the top of the Hancock Tower, to my Aunt Susan's, to Joffrey Ballet's *The Nutcracker*, and on a tour of Frank Lloyd Wright's home and studio.

At the Fairmont Hotel, our rooms were on the twelfth floor, and each had large picture windows, two over-stuffed sitting chairs, and a writing desk. As usual, the rooms were separated by a common door, the kids in one, Anna and I in the other—or so we thought.

The fun started with the kids wrangling over who would get which bed. Without too much haggling, they worked it out. Sofia slept in one of the beds with Adam, but because Hanna insisted on sleeping alone, she ordered a rollaway bed for Olivia.

And then, before I could say, "What's for dinner?" the adjoining door swung open, and the kids paraded into our room, one by one. My and Anna's privacy was no more. Our only prayer was that we could sleep by ourselves—probably not a chance.

It didn't take long for the migration to become permanent. In short order, Sofia suggested menus, followed by playful guest services, and then took drink orders that were served from the mini bar. Olivia insisted on taking her showers in our bathroom. Hanna used both vanity mirrors. Adam raised hell with his sisters, insisting that they fully understand his big-brother status when it came to sleeping arrangements. Of course, Anna was the proprietor of the candy store, guarding the sweets, hiding them as if they were gold. And, dare I say, it appeared as if she was eating most of them too.

But there was no room for complaints. Families are all about sharing. So it was that our two rooms become one joined by a marble threshold—our retreat for the days to come.

I was the first to get out of bed on Saturday morning. It was still dark when I opened the curtains and stared out at life in the big city through high-rise glass windows. Wherever I looked were thousands of windows just like ours, some lit, but most dark. For a moment I was Jimmy Stewart in Hitchcock's *Rear Window*, imagining a story lurking behind each pane of glass. And there was a story behind the very glass that was reflecting the image of me in boxers looking out at the city with two roomfuls of stories behind me.

City high-rise watching can be interesting. It was eerie and thrilling watching each lit window: A Christmas tree, a counterpart sitting in a chair, or far below, the early-morning walkers all bundled up against the cold, and cars moving carefully across the icy roads.

And it was at that precise moment that I felt the chill of the winter weather.

Our first morning turned out to be a special one. Snow

had fallen throughout the night, covering everything to a white horizon. The street lights were still on, and the falling snow sparkled under the glow of their bright yellow lamps.

Feeling selfish for enjoying this treat by myself, I woke Olivia, my normal early-riser. We quickly got dressed, and headed for the great outdoors.

The cold slammed into us as soon as we exited the revolving doors, but we were filled with joy as the snowflakes fell on our tongues. Realizing that we were having too much fun just for the two of us, we returned to get Sofia. Of course, I couldn't help but wonder if she would simply be the target of Olivia's snowballs, or would she team up with her to take out her Papa? No matter, for I knew this was going to be an extraordinary morning. And indeed it was, for in short order we were walking the empty streets—snowballs flying, the previously untouched snow patches were soon marked with footprints and snow angels.

Soon, the rest of the family was awake and eager to join in. We built a snowman, and the doorman assured us that he'd guard it with his life. Our morning walk took us over an arctic windblown bridge to a stainless-steel moose, where Anna spoke glowingly about her brother Jan's love for this particular breed of animal.

It was a great day to be in this winter wonderland known as Chicago. But then our joy was somewhat smothered because of ...well, as all of us knew, family matters were to creep in since we'd planned to visit Aunt Susan, my mother's sister, that afternoon.

Because I had not spoken with Susan for almost a decade, not since my grandmother's death, I anticipated, with some trepidation, introducing our children to her and her husband, John. The kids were equally as anxious because Susan and John were somewhat of a mystery—familiar names without faces.

When we arrived at Susan and John's house, every room was carefully decorated for Christmas, and their tree was two stories tall. While introductions were made and coffee shared,

John and Susan quickly endeared themselves to our children with their humor and gentleness. Susan almost immediately presented them with a plate in hand: "Kids, I have some cookies and candies. Would you like some?"

Shortly thereafter, we had lunch out at a local restaurant. And that's when complications set in.

With the kids outside playing in the snow, the waiter cleared the plates, asked if we wanted dessert. We ordered, he brought something, and that's when Susan and I struck up a long-overdue conversation—pretenses and relatives' dishonesty be damned.

Susan asked, "How's your mother doing?"

"The same, still drinking. I don't see her much when I go to San Diego. We have lunch, but it's been years. Lynn and James are good, though." I couldn't help myself and followed with questions about Susan and my mother's brother, David. I'd always been curious about David's death. When I was about ten years old, I was told what seemed to be a far-fetched story, a story I'd never questioned because it was repeated hundreds of times over the years by both my mother and father and my grandmother. The story went that while Uncle David was serving in Vietnam with the Navy, he'd fallen in love with a local girl, and she was a Communist. It became impossible for David and his lover to reunite in the United States due to her political affiliations, so David killed himself in my grandmother's basement.

When I asked Susan about all of this, given all those years of living with a single explanation, I was floored to hear her reply. "Nothing could be further from the truth—David was gay. His suicide was from the stress and anxiety about his being gay and being gay in the Navy."

Her reply had this bluntness about it, like I should have known how common this humiliation was, as if her brother's death was an acceptable solution to such prejudice. What a desperate scheme it must have all been. Perhaps they all sat around and agreed early on that children should not hear such things.

I was stunned beyond words. My chest tightened. I took a deep breath as images flashed back to my mother and grandparents telling me the elaborate set of falsehoods. I chewed on all the lies, it all came back to me. I was further incensed right then. I needed to tell my sister and brother immediately, I thought. How could they do that to their son? How could my mother do that to her brother? How selfish they all were to not at least try to understand David's lifestyle. It was incomprehensible to conceal the truth for so long, and hide behind their shame and under a blanket of deceit. It was despicable. It put them in the same league as those who persecuted him because of who he was. I wanted to tell Susan of my disapproval, but I just went silent and asked for the check.

It should be a given that parents teach their children not to lie, but that didn't happen for me. They lied to me, and I lied to them. Those everyday lies, promises of nothings, the cover-ups became instinctive in our home. Growing up with them, they became truths. Now, I know the truths.

During the ride back to the hotel, I told the kids the story about Uncle David. My shame had nothing to do about his lifestyle, and everything to do with speaking the truth, rebuking those falsehoods that hurt so deeply for generations. Although I wasn't sure if and when we would visit Aunt Susan as a family again, I hoped we would. I did know that my children clearly saw the importance of truthful family exchanges and the long-lasting damage that lies could generate.

18 Our Winter Nightmare

December 15, 2007

The evening started out pleasant enough, except for the truth that was spoken in so few words. We were dressed in our finest suits and ties, dresses and fancy shoes. We loaded into the hotel's Bentley. Across the street sat a firehouse and construction site lit up for Christmas. The driver made rights and lefts, and we soon arrived at the theater. As we watched *The Nutcracker*, Mother Nature decided to play one of her jokes on us by dumping several inches of snow on Chicago.

Because there were no taxicabs in sight when we left the theater, we were simply carried along with the crowd. Of course, we had no idea where we were going, and soon were alone and lost. Even scarier, the city seemed to have shut down. Snow, wind and bitter cold added to our confusion. As we made our way down a dimly-lit downtown side street, I tried to open any and all doors or find someone to ask directions. But then a city bus drove past, slowed, and stopped. We ran toward it—the only sign of life in the weather-beaten city. The driver saw we were lost and frightened and asked if we needed help.I said, "We're lost and nearly frozen. We're trying to get to the Fairmont Hotel."

The man was comforting. He gave us an encouraging smile and, in a gentle voice, "C'mon in and have a seat and warm yourself up. I'll get you close."

After about five minutes of warmth, the bus came to a halt. "This is your stop. Walk about a block to that tunnel door," he said, pointing the way. "That tunnel will take you to the Fairmont Hotel. Good luck."

Anna, Sofia, Olivia, Hanna, Adam and I each thanked

him as we stepped off the bus and into a blinding flurry of snow. Our journey began again—one agonizing step at a time. As we slowly made our way to the underground passageway door, I struggled against the freezing wind, my hands and face numbed in no time at all.

Adam was the first to reach the door. He tried the handle, but it didn't turn. "It's locked," he yelled.

I pointed across an expansive courtyard and up a flight of stairs, where a security guard was patrolling a high-rise lobby—our lighthouse.

"Up there. That guard will help us, he'll tell us how to get to the hotel," I told the kids.

We trudged up the stairs, unable to avoid the horizontal snow. We pushed against the bitter wind toward the building's glass entryway, which was attached to the lobby through a set of revolving doors. It was there that the guard stood when we began our trek. But he was gone.

We all banged on the glass doors. We shouted for help, but no one answered. Sofia was frightened. Olivia, wearing simple sandals, complained that her feet and ankles were freezing. Hanna was acting like a lost deer prancing in the snow.

Chaos had set in.

Anna kept a clear head, though. My Swede wasn't about to let a little snow and wintry chill ruin her night. She gathered the kids about her and laid down the law. "Do not move from here," she told them. "I'm going out to look around. Don't move."

And then Anna disappeared into the storm.

Concerned for her safety, I walked as far out into the snow-covered courtyard as I could and still keep an eye on our group. I gave her a shout, but she didn't reappear. My uncertainty grew, but then I looked around and noticed the construction site that was familiar, and heard the bleating siren from a fire-truck. I knew I recognized this place—our hotel was just across the street.

"Come here! Come here!" I yelled to the kids, and they

promptly came at a run. I told Adam, "Take your sisters down one block, and turn left. I'll go find Mama."

Adam complied, and I prayed our snowman was still there, standing guard to guide him and the girls safely to our hotel.

But then another problem arose. Sofia refused to go with Adam and her sisters. She stood steadfast beside me, concern etched on her face. I shouted for Anna once again, and now my other prayer was answered as she materialized from out of the snow-speckled dark.

We trudged along the same path Adam, Hanna and Olivia had taken to find the hotel ahead, and there were our children peering out at us through the glass walls of the Fairmont lobby.

Safe and sound inside the Fairmont, over dinner there was lots of talk about individual acts of bravery and how, as a family, we came face-to-face with Mother Nature's wrath and conquered a nightmare.

Later, as Anna and the kids sampled the sweets back at our room's candy store, all the while marveling that their valiant snowman was still standing guard at the hotel's entranceway, I savored the merriment and breathed a sign of weary relief.

Chicago was where my mother and father grew up, went to school and married, which led me back beneath the surface of all the stories I'd heard growing up. I agonized about the real nightmare—there was no escaping the past.

Mother's lies and her self-pity following her brother's death imploded her world. After her father died, her mother and sister did not speak to her, and Mom resents them deeply still, with no reason for it that I can tell. David's death and Mom's deceit were the diversion that gave her an excuse to drink and run around on Dad, which caused their divorce, an act that subsequently shattered our childhood. It was her cab ride to hell, as she turned on herself and her family and replaced us with vodka and prescription drugs. I wanted her to crash; bury her and the past like some cat in the backyard. I was sick of the fear, the lack of peace. My childhood was a place where pride was stripped away to embarrassment, where it was impossible to imagine anything but the hang-over of confusion and spite, and where survival became my perception of what was family. Here the good and the bad were not much different, so I tried to make up the good.

But there was always something still ahead, a place where you could wake up fresh, open a window and watch from behind the tinted glass. A Swedish woman appeared in white shorts, on some beach, where she took off her clothes. I watched. She had a clear understanding of her emotions, and wanted new experiences that were so dissimilar to mine. That look behind the glass was a welcomed reality.

19 Southern Oaks

December 31, 2007

We met the Morans down on Saint Simon Island, Georgia for the New Year, a place that less than two years later, I and my family would return to in a different life.

On the last morning of 2007, I walked over to a patch of oak trees to just have some quiet time. Most everyone was still asleep. I let Anna know where I was going, and she said she would drop by in the car after everyone was up and their morning started. As I sat there, I wrote the first draft of this chapter. Tim read it later that evening with some enthusiasm, which encouraged me to write more. It wasn't meant to be a metaphor for anything really, though it could be. I just wanted to write something about that old family of trees, we have so much in common with them, and these trees were so full of poetry as they poured shade over me.

Sitting at the edge of the marsh of a Southern bayou, resting on the roots in the shade of the oaks is a pleasant way to spend the final hours of the year.

These oaks are several hundred years old. Their roots corkscrew into the sandy dirt, springing up here and there, but they secure the trees' massive weight. Other than their beauty, what I find amazing is that they sprang from a simple seed—nourished only by sunlight and water to become giants in a hardwood forest.

Wherever I look, dense underbrush gives homes to birds, squirrels and countless other small creatures. And the ground below the oaks is covered with decaying leaves, which covers even more seeds, some of which will sprout on their own someday.

The trees' thick trunks are the statues of this forest. Their rough, vein-like bark provides a perfect habitat for light green lichen. High above, solid limbs extend in all directions, reaching out branch-by-branch, and twig-by-twig.

And, as if the Almighty chose to garland these special specimens, gray sea-grass drapes over fern-covered limbs, dense clusters withering to single strands.

Here, nature's tinsel hangs gently, its curtains swaying softly in the wind—the epitome of ole' Southern charm within this oak forest by the sea.

20 A Spring Morning

April 2, 2008

The day I turned fifty, a milestone of sorts—half-young, hopefully; half-old, perhaps more likely—something got me to thinking of 1976—the year I was a senior in high school, determined to strike out on my own. All that stood in my way was the means. One thing was for certain—I couldn't rely on my father or mother for support. They were too wrapped up in their own pursuits; all they were concerned about was running away from themselves and each other.

I viewed my childhood and our family life, or lack of one, as a life-lesson: Mix two parts insensitivity with an overabundance of selfishness, and you've created dysfunction to the Nth degree (sounds a bit like one of Mom's cocktail recipes). Let this simmer over a given number of years, and by then everyone had developed a sixth-sense, which enabled each of us to run for cover.

Dad was the first to scurry away from the pressure, moving to San Francisco, where he inherited a second family when he remarried. He took Lynn with him. In hindsight, I believe that this separation from Mother rescued Lynn. He was protecting his only daughter, and I get that, it's a whole different thing in my experience. Sons must take care of themselves, and daughters, they rely on fathers for that insurance, that protection, or should be able to. Lynn, in particular, was important to Dad. She was young and had been less affected and less aware of the bad. He could make meaning there, which he did.

With me and James, it was different. Dad visited us one weekend. He came wearing his suit, gave me the check to cover the first month's rent for an apartment and food. Money was so important to him, if I ripped it up and threw it in his face, I knew this grand gesture of his would never happen again, so I just took it. I thought we were back in his life, that we now had a value.

I wouldn't miss coming home to the smell of the vodka, the tables of half-empty glasses or that image of my mother spread out, legs open, face planted down on the pillow-less bed. But looking back, Dad had made money his mission. Though something must have been piling up for him where we were concerned, and we became a buy-out, leveraged by his guilt. The bleeding was covered with a band-aid in the form of an investment that he could write down, a transaction of buy and sell. But I was thankful for my father's gesture because I was out of both of their lives, a teenager on his own.

Unfortunately, James was unable to cut the cord, so he moved back in with Mom after only a few months. It proved to be one of those uncanny déjà vus. Decades from that day when he'd moved away from that little apartment we'd shared, and in his late forties, he became hooked on prescription opiates and rum and lost his wife and three children as a result. He spent his inheritance and time in strip bars, and he moved back in with his mother. His new girlfriends were in the business of providing pleasure, drugs and addictions as long as he could pay for them. They buried him in meth, keeping him close while they drained his bank account of close to $100,000. He resorted to selling his final possessions to keep the party going. He lost his house, his children's respect and what was once a sharp mind. He lived on the streets in his car for awhile. It must have been disappointing to have spent that first night back in his mother's home, living in some shit hole that he'll probably never escape.

My children could have remembered their uncle as sober, and they'd not seen him his since his plunge. They knew about his addictions, how it ran in the family. But James began calling my kids, saying horrible things, "Your father's a drug dealer and addict too," all to justify his own addictions. He told them I was a terrible brother and uncle, and that I was a loud, insensitive, self-serving asshole with no pity for his "medical condition." I'd been a part of the party in the seventies, but I'd determined that I wouldn't be like Mom, and now like him. James was trying to turn my kids against me, like his kids had turned on him, like James and I had turned on our father. My kids were smart enough to stop taking his calls, and that's how they left him. My sister and I tried to get him to rehab, but when he jumped out of the moving car on the freeway onramp and weeks later broke into my sister's house, we gave up. His family situation and his perceptions of mine and Lynn's seemed to fuel his anger.

When I returned to San Diego on a business trip a few months later, I took Mom and James to that Grotto restaurant of our youth; we saw other families, heard merry voices of children playing, the quack of ducks, and the splash of water falling. I thought, looking around at all those families, this was now happiness, this was life, or I hoped so, anyway. We mostly just sat silently for a while, then ate. It had been a struggle in my heart to forgive my unhappy brother and mother. I wished I could have assisted them, but I knew it was impossible to do that. I asked if there was anything troubling them—though I had no right to ask them that. James had difficulty understanding what I was talking about, and it was as if the external world had deprived him of perception. James hardly spoke at all. His eyes were empty, deep wells of dull light. He started defending Mother's way of life, which was when he became a child again—together with his dear mother, their relationship one that I will never wish to comprehend. The two had fallen into despair, I could see that their hopes were gone. There was no sense of enjoyment as they pushed the empty plates away. James, with his quivering voice, got up slowly, then worked his mind to say, "Goodbye."

That morning of my fiftieth birthday, I thought of my past—of that spring in 1976, when my father set me free, made me hard. I did not want to brood about growing up, though Dad had forced me to find the unknown, by that I mean self-respect, while forgetting the kind of journey it took to go from being a boy to a man. I wanted to make sure my children would never go through that kind of adversity, that their home would be a place they'd always want to return to, a place where Anna would always be making food for her babies, a place where we could sit around a table, nestle under a blanket, recounting times or just talking out loud.

With sunlight illuminating our white bedroom through gauze curtains, I turned to glance at my wife. Anna was still asleep, her face a picture of serenity. And nestled ever-so-lightly in her arms was Oliver. His forepaws resting on Anna's forearm, his eyes were tightly shut, his breathing timed to the beat of his heart. Both were at rest, each seemingly keeping the other asleep.

Small noises—a grumble in the breathing, a movement of an arm, a turn of a shoulder—signs of agitation. And then Anna's breathing quickened, her eyes opened on the dawn of a new day. Her movements were slow and forced.

Outside our open window, the sun warmed the chilled air. As the treetops held close the sunlight, the sounds of rustling leaves and occasional raindrops served as nature's wake-up call. Gentle light spilled radiance. Closed tulips would open to embrace dawn as it became day, lighter to bright, until the flowers turned crimson.

Carols of birds stirred up the forest; one bird sang louder than all the others. Squirrels descended trees, then scampered along the forest floor for fallen nuts. Flacken prowled, aroused by new smells carried on the air.

As was the custom of creatures and nature in the early hours of dawn, movement was everywhere.

And then the light filled each room of our house, which woke the kids for their daily routines.

Anna opened a side door, allowing the morning freshness to pour in. She slowly put on rubber boots and walked over wet grass toward the stables, where the horses were restless. She unlocked the heavy metal locks, swung open the barn doors, letting the horses out to run toward their breakfast of damp grass.

Back in the house, the kids' feet were heavy on the floors and stairs. Sofia sleepily shifted ever-so-slowly toward the sofa, where she disappeared under more blankets. Anna started up the coffee maker, began to rustle around in the refrigerator, the cabinets—Adam would be starving. The girls would pick at their breakfasts while Anna urged them to eat.

One by one, these were our routines on spring mornings.

But like stones in old rivers flowing south, the winds of the day always hurried us along to school, and work and the everyday.

21 Pittsburgh, Pennsylvania

May 17, 2008

We came to this city of steel and glass to see Bill and Carol Burnell—old acquaintances. Although we had not seen them for some time, ours was one of those friendships that transcended time—generations, to be exact.

Twenty years earlier, Anna and I had been married at the Burnells' San Diego home. Anna was the Burnells' Swedish au-pair who cared for Bill and Carol's four-year-old son Derek and their daughter Melissa.

This time, with our own four children in tow, we were in Pittsburgh to witness Derek Burnell's marriage to Jess, his bride-to-be.

We arrived on Thursday to this city bound by two rivers. Testimony to Pittsburgh's glorious past was the vast array of steel bridges. Rolling along the landscape were the Alleghany

Mountains, with their light-green backdrop of hardwoods. And dotting the hillsides were brick houses, wooded barns and silos. This was farm country—home to hard-working folks whose priorities were raising families and livestock.

The city itself was a mix of the old and new. In the past, it was the old moguls of industry—Carnegie, Mellon, Frick and Kauffman—who made this city one of the nation's leaders of commerce. Now, rows of brown strip-warehouses had been converted to shops, each with an intrinsic tie to the area's European antiquity, despite being intermixed within glass high-rises. In this diversity lay the heart of Pittsburgh's citizens and culture.

We stayed at the Renaissance, one of the city's old establishments on Sixth Street, in the heart of the theater district. It was a fine hotel with a grand, marble lobby and an expansive staircase crowned by a scalloped glass-and-wood skylight.

As usual, our rooms were connected. And once again, Adam was bunking with Sofia. Indeed, Adam enjoyed his big-brother role. Hanna, however, wasn't quite as eager to embrace her position as big sister, but after a bit of coaxing, when Olivia agreed to not move when sleeping, Hanna let her share the bed. It was a bit taxing to see sisterly bonding in the making.

Our first evening was spent catching up on lost time with Bill and Carol, plus reacquainting ourselves with Derek and Melissa, both of whom had grown into remarkable adults. We hadn't seen them since they were children. Bill had his own law firm, and Carol was an accountant, but their professions had nothing to do with who they were. Carol outran age with her beauty; Bill had lost most his hair, but his laugh made up for that. They seemed so settled in good ways. They recalled all the happiness that Anna's Swedish gang of girls brought to their house. Bill seemed to recall more than Carol and with good reason. We picked up right where we left off, but with our gang of four kids along for the stories.

As the evening drifted along, our list of newfound friends grew—sisters, grandparents and cousins. Seeing everyone across the table where food and wine were in abundance was wonderful. We listened to all these sincere sentiments about family, about the couple and their parents—these people loved and were loved in return.

After an evening of Italian food and a few spirited beverages, we returned to the hotel, intent on relaxation. But as we sat down to watch an in-room movie, the fire alarm screamed, so off we scurried. It was a false alarm, of course, but there we found ourselves with the rest of the hotel guests—all of us milling around outside the building in robes and pajamas, and sleepy-eyed. The fire trucks arrived and departed, leaving all of us with another tale to share with friends back home.

The next morning we were greeted by rain. No matter. Nothing was going to stop me from having my family see the finest piece of architecture on the planet—the home of the Pittsburgh department store mogul Edgar J. Kaufmann, designed by Frank Lloyd Wright. Our destination was approximately an hour's drive from the city—over the riveted steel bridges, past sculptured mountains—to a place of water, trees and organic grandeur.

Our next stop, I told Anna and the gang, was Falling Water.

22 Falling Water

May 17, 2008

As we walked down the trail, it was not the sky—the wash of blues or the way the light split the tree branches—it was the rushing water running over boulders that overpowered us. There was a certain sound to these echoes—the unmistakable roar of water cascading violently over and around rock as if escaping from underground. And crossing over a bridged driveway, we saw the concrete structure hanging precariously over the river like some tight-rope walker balanced over a canyon, where his pole provides a sense of what appears to be unsteadied stability.

It was a sight that would give even the most jaded of tourists pause—I wanted to take it in for what it was, one of the most recognized structures in the world, balanced within nature. But, in this instance, it was not the extraordinary manmade structure that shook my subconscious—it was the mere act of crossing over to where one man's achievement was established, the place where he discovered what his life would be.

Some of the best times of my teenage years were spent on the back of an AJS-250 Stormer, my kick-ass, two-cycle engine dirt bike. In truth, that bike was the only uncomplicated thing about my life. I was fourteen, the year was 1972. Dad was gone. James, Lynn and I were the family. Mom would come and go with Lynn mostly to ice skate. Lynn was very good at skating. She flowed and drifted like falling snow.

I'd get home and throw the school books down, shake the bike for gas, turn on the petcock, and jump start the engine as I rolled down the steep hill we lived on. Thank God gas was cheap. I had to mix oil with the fuel, and I loved the smell of the engine exhaust when I barreled down our street toward the end of the asphalt. It was at this point, in the blurred blink of an eye that I'd cross over—escaping at full-throttle. It was my daily routine, and out on the dirt trails my friends, Ron, Craig and Scott would show up on their bikes. We hauled ass, made noise and crashed now and then until darkness fell on the hills.

Granted, it was always a mindless journey, hell-bent-for-whatever over hundreds of acres of shrubs, twisting and turning along trails leading to nowhere, just away—gone. I'd ride for hours, the excursions ending only when I ran out of gas or when the cops finally came close to tracking us down, which forced us back home.

Cops were a pain. They were big into handing out citations for rides down the neighborhood streets, excessive noise or no registration. Of course, what irked them the most was the trespassing, which we did on a regular basis.

The cops were always harassing bikers at a great cost to them too. They'd use helicopters to track our movements, then radio patrol officers, who'd try to run us down on their Swedish Husqvarna dirt bikes. In hindsight, I don't know who had the most fun—us or the cops. Whenever we'd spot their dust clouds closing in, we'd hit the throttle and zigzag our way down a couple of trails, then race to someone's home and ditch the bikes in the garage, locking the door behind us.

Beating the law was easy—simply a matter of not answering the door when they rang the bell.

The only thing that truly bothered me was why those cops focused so much of their attention on us kids. I mean, there was pot growing all over those hills, not to mention illegal immigrants strolling along wherever you looked.

No matter, those were good years of fun and games—outrunning the law, we zipped across acre after acre, occasionally coming across a home situated in the hills and making our unwelcomed acquaintance. Landowners resorted to barbwire fences erected on t-steel posts. No sweat; we'd just clip the wire. They'd replace it; we'd just cut it again.

But it was neither the homeowners nor the cops that brought an end to my Easy Rider days. The culprit was my mother and her fascination with emptying and hiding bottles around the house.

She took out a second mortgage on the house, as well as on us kids. Hers was a seamless plan. Once the money and the booze ran out and she needed to unload the house, she did just that, avoiding the embarrassment of having to place a "For Sale" sign in the front yard. It did not matter to her, but the house was the only stable thing to us. She made her excuses. "We have to sell the house—your father won't up the child-support payments. He's such an asshole." So she sold the house silently and quickly, one of the benefits of her being a realtor.

Her boozing was no secret. The neighbors knew what was going on; they most likely wanted us all gone anyway.

The day of my last ride for good, I was feeling sorry for myself, full of thought and close to a meltdown, I jumped on the bike—no helmet, my long hair blowing in the wind—and zoomed to the top of Explore Road. I killed the engine with a press of a black button, all was silent.

Revelation is a scary thing, no matter how old you are. At that moment, I knew there was no one I could count on—not that I hadn't been close to getting this before. Everything clicked into place. All the evidence finally jelled or perhaps I was just facing it. I knew my past would get me nowhere, and I needed to find my own way now. I was Columbus discovering the new world—my new world.

I realized now I'd be able to stomp the brakes on this rollercoaster. I was struck with a newfound self-assurance or call it clarity of stupidity. I finally knew survival meant separating from the nothing I was living for, from the nowhere I lived, in order to discover who exactly I was meant to be. This was not an easy choice for a fourteen-year-old, yet a necessary choice, and it hardened me inside in the right way.

Adam was seventeen when we went to Falling Water. I stood there with him next to a small pond, just to the right of a narrow doorway. The sounds of its dripping water were magnified by the pond's channeled surrounding, which were in contrast to the sounds of the cascading waterfalls. We stepped through a tight doorway and hall and up, then into an expansive living space. It was magnificent.

What greeted us was the stone—all balanced on a cantilevered structure dangling over a raging river and falls. Wright's genius allowed the outside in. How metaphoric of him to think of such a thing—as if he knew some secret he was trying to show everyone about how one should live. But the truth is, while he may have had an inkling about letting the outside in, he couldn't live by that either.

That extraordinary room had a stone floor of waxed river rocks, which gave visitors the impression of navigating eroded and misty river stones. The stones beckoned the eye up and along stacked-stone walls and out through glass walls. A rounded boulder protruded through the floor, near the fireplace as if holding the floating room in place. A Wright-designed steel kettle of bright red hung next to the fireplace, reminding us not only of our human needs, but also of our past.

Narrow, right-angled stairs rose from the corner of the room toward dark corridors, which, in turn, led to private quarters.

Low ceilings and a maze of dim passages led to bedrooms. Although the master bedroom was larger and more private, each of the other rooms was a work of structural art, as if they were floating like some helium balloons, complete with a private veranda surrounded by forest, held up by invisible strings attached to heaven.

Another set of stairs took us up to the third floor, a crow's nest set of rooms designed for children to play in isolation from their parents.

The horizontal detail of the paneled-wood walls and protruding shelves directed my eyes toward forest, shadows and light. These windows, when open, amplified the sound of the ever-present water, and seemed to disappear into vertical sight-lines within themselves.

There was an almost unworldly exactness to each space in the house as well as on the grounds.

Every detail was conscientiously defined by light, sound, material and location—all conceived to meld man as one with nature. And in this place, I flashed back to when I found my solitude, where I would achieve something great—nurture a family.

23 The Marriage

May 18, 2008

Days such as those were the best of times—a bright morning sun, crisp spring air, and everyone embracing an upbeat spirit as we prepared for Derek Burnell and Jess's big wedding.

Our own preparations began with Adam's command, "Okay, it's time to suit up."

At just seventeen, Adam had already acquired a fine eye for detail. He smiled approvingly as he admired his new brown suit, dress shirt and my silk tie in the mirror. Perfection, I thought…well, almost.

He fumbled with his tie, couldn't get the knot to look skinny. I waited until he asked.

"Can't get the knot right, can you do this for me?"

Now how do you respond to a statement like that? "You've got to learn to do this for yourself soon." I stepped over to him, lifting the shirt's collar and adjusted the tie lengths around his neck, flipped the tie in my hands while explaining the proper way to tie a Windsor. When the knot was complete, Adam checked the length and thanked me as he admired himself again. His, at that moment, was the look of a well-dressed teenager rapidly growing into a man. Someday my ties would be his ties.

In short order, Hanna stepped to the mirror. Our eldest daughter had a mind and quick wit that worked nonstop. Her beauty was one of reluctance. She liked to play it down with simple dress, straight hair, parted to emphasize her in-charge, smart appearance.

Hanna surveyed any and all situations for a precise understanding before she allowed herself to react. Her always-questioning nature caused her much hesitation. Her long, dark hair was naturally curly, yet she insisted on straightening it. Her narrow nose sat perfectly between green eyes, with a perfect mouth and perfect lips, which hid perfect white teeth that were occasionally displayed with a smile of self-controlled joy.

Ah, but at the wedding, Hanna planned to look like a princess.

While Anna, Hanna, and Olivia worked on their hair, they helped Sofia just enough to not slow down their own progress. And although I was merely a spectator, unable to help in these rituals, I listened, amused at the dialogue between the ladies of the house: "I need the hair dryer…Can I get in there?" It went on and on, back and forth, broken often by Olivia's persistent, "How's this look?" as she changed from one dress to another.

Sofia took it all in, quietly watching her older sisters and mother go through the lengthy process of getting ready. And then, without further word, she simply got dressed, following big brother's lead.

Finally ready, we rode the elevator to the lobby to greet the wedding party and to then board the waiting cars, which took us to the Phipps Conservatory and Botanical Gardens for the ceremony.

We found seats among the white chairs set in precise rows, the aisle cutting down the middle. The wedding party walked down looking so blissful, and the groom and his boys, slightly drunk, having settled in the hotel bar earlier. The pastor waited as the cameras clicked, and we all stood as the bride moved down the passage of the family and friends. Most of us were quiet, except for that one tiny infant you always come across at weddings—the baby who's fussing and crying a bit, calling the subconscious cue to those in attendance, though it was more of a trigger for those of us who have children because we know what it's like to hold the screamer. I guess when you exchange vows, a baby's cry is the last thing you hear, that is unless your bride is in her second trimester, which wasn't the case with Jess.

As with all weddings, there was no room large enough to contain the pride of the wedding couple's parents, and those of us who had children that were getting near that age were affected too. Tears filled the mothers' eyes. Fathers stood tall. And all about the sanctuary, a stillness descended upon the crowd as the bride and groom exchanged their solemn words—we were hushed as though we all uttered those words too, from our heart of hearts, our profound desire that this commitment of love would endure.

Such were our hopes and prayers for the young couple's success—I reflected on my own marriage—its successes and failures, and I thought that the other married folks there did the same. And looking at my kids, I wondered if the girls were envisioning themselves looking like Jess—radiant, beautiful, happy. And then, Adam, looking more grown up than I'd seen him. I thought he must have been picturing Stephanie and imagining their own wedding, honeymoon, children.

And then with the speed that I guess only God could command, rain clouds appeared over the ceremony. But, with the vows completed, everyone scurried to the indoor gardens to the reception—all of us hungry, most looking forward to a drink. The tables had been arranged, and small gifts sat in front our place cards that had been scripted in calligraphy.

Bars throughout the garden were heavily attended, mostly by the wedding party at first, while waiters served hors d'oeuvres on silver plates amid the steady rumble of excited guests, who eagerly shared with each other their personal highlights of the ceremony. Adam and my girls were people-watching as they opened the gifts of Swiss chocolate. We were overwhelmed with the attention to detail, all the little arrangements that we were breathing in.

As usual, the seating arrangements were the work of someone's well-intentioned idea of enhancing dinner conversation and which, most oftentimes, are based on someone's idea of you or preconception of who you are and what you're like. Do they think you're exciting, boring, or are you in the stupid section? In this case, the hosts got it right—much to our surprise and delight, Anna and I were seated at the same table as the pastor and his wife. We complimented the pastor for his words at the wedding, for this rite of passage. He smiled, thanked us, but oddly his wife didn't respond, just kept to herself.

We continued making small talk and trying to bring her into the conversation. My and Anna's eyes met repeatedly, saying to the other that we both had the same sense of this woman who hadn't spoken much. She had childlike expressions on her face as if clinging to him was her role that day. I thought I should speak to her plainly. What did it all mean? Why was she so reluctant? It soon became obvious to Anna and me that the pastor's wife was that sort of troublesome itch you just can't scratch, the irritating pebble in your shoe that you're in the wrong place to remove. In short, she was just overbearing—dictated his every move with slight gestures, instructing him to get her food; and he required her approvals. She set his napkin on his lap, and constantly found fault with everything large and small. Thus, an uncomfortable silence settled over our table—as if that rain cloud earlier was back.

In a final attempt to engage the pastor's wisdom, I asked, "Where do you stand on the subject of gay marriage?" Always a hot-button issue, and maybe, given the pastor's wife, not the best of questions for the situation. I just asked about it to make conversation and because I was curious. It was at a time when such issues were in the news every day, and most people were still formulating a position.

Of course, the kids were a bit shocked by my bluntness. It was their first time dining with a man of the cloth, and they didn't expect heavy conversation. But as I said, I was curious. After all, not only had California recently passed the gay rights marriage act, but it was no secret there were gay couples at this joyous occasion, including some in the wedding party, and I was determined to defend Uncle David, even if a generation late.

The pastor, who, to my mind, should be a man of peace,

smiled and said, "I know the Church does not sanction these relationships, but it seems okay with me."

His wife gave him a look, then retorted, "Fine, now we can all be miserable." Meaning what, exactly?

That certainly put a quick end to any further conversation. And after a few minutes of the pastor's wife fidgeting with her purse, conveying her disgust, the pastor stood and announced, "We have to leave for another commitment."

As I watched them leave, I shifted my gaze to the head table, where several gay couples sat—adorned in their gowns and suits, sharing their laughter, being warmly received by family, friends and guests.

Our friends and Derek and Jess stopped by our table to express their gratitude for our coming and helping make the event special. While our family embraced these sentiments, I couldn't help but think of the pastor's wife and how visible was her blindness to the happiness that was in the room, straight or gay.

24 Gothenburg, Sweden

June–July, 2008

I find no joy in being separated from my family, but so that the family can have more time abroad, Anna and the kids leave weeks before I can travel, then we all return home together. There are even those trips she makes, which I can't follow her on at all, and those are the most stressful. While a phone call can provide a buffer against absolute solitude, it is a poor substitute for the playfulness and joy that home brings when the family's around.

So, there I was walking about an empty house, my family thousands of miles away in Sweden. The curse of fathers worldwide—the job—kept me from making the trip several weeks earlier with Anna, Adam, Hanna, Olivia and Sofia. But I was packing my bags to join them.

The house was dark, and the things which normally gave me so much pleasure, my bookshelves filled with Hemingway and Fitzgerald, poetry; my congas; the girls' violins (which they'd been neglecting lately) seemed to all belong to another person, to someone who used to live here. I wondered if my father had looked at his house, the house where his wife, his children were no longer his—dispossessed of what he'd worked for, established, made. The children had left strewn about all the odds and ends that they'd rejected when packing, and again, the feeling of all this belonging to someone else rose in me.

I had to say good-bye to Oliver and Flacken. I had been with them for weeks without words; the only communication simply low purrs and tail-wags. They were keenly aware I was the only member of the family present, and they showed me great affection. Of course, Oliver was most upset while he watched me prepare to abandon him—no tail-wagging. He followed me everywhere with the guilt-trip pet owners know well—sad eyes and drooping ears—he tried his best to persuade me to take him along.

Leaving Oliver and Flacken with the neighbors, I scurried off to the airport. Next stop: Gothenburg, Sweden.

In a moment of hindsight, I realized we had not been to Gothenburg as a family for nearly twelve years. It was long overdue, so I was going to make the very best of it. And after what seemed like a slow overseas flight, I was greeted at the airport by Anna, Hanna and Sofia. Our reuniting was a godsend for me. I had missed Anna's kiss, Hanna's curious smile and Sofia's hugs.

We drove straight to a party place called The Palace, where revelers ate and drank long into the night. Anna's brother, Jan, whose recent stroke caused much pain and sorrow in the family, was the celebrity architect who designed this establishment. We no sooner sat down to lunch when Anna's phone rang; in her native Swedish she assured the person on the other line that I'd gotten there safe and sound, perhaps a little road weary, but glad.

These trips to Sweden involved us spending time with Anna's relatives, which always provided an honest education, enacted with daily drama that was both significant and insignificant. We always resided at Anna's mother house; Siv is an angel put here on earth to watch over family. Siv's husband Valdemar Vasilis passed away years ago, and lays at rest in the family plot not far from Uggelboda. Siv has four children: Maria Vasilis Brändstöm is the oldest daughter, and the most likely to give advice, and her husband Erik Brändstöm is an air force major who likes to captain small boats when fishing. Jan Vasilis is Siv's only son and is on a second marriage, to "Little Eva" who is one of those bombshells that we all imagine on the Swedish Olympic swim team. Eva Vasilis Nilsson is Siv's second daughter. She is also an angel and married to Bengt Nilsson, who is lost in some aristocratic dream no one understands and wouldn't be considered in any kind of guardian category. Then there are Siv's grandchildren (not including my and Anna's children): Martin, Magus, Linnea, Emlie, Elin, Julia, Jontan, and Amanda, all principled people at various stages of growing up, where they are restless, masculine, feminine, ambitious, but most of all take part in the affairs worth living for. And my dear Anna is Siv's baby girl by birthright, and is married to me. As for where I fit in: It's in this place where poetic luck and lust for pleasures lie, a place where we can make meaning, but a place from which we will ultimately transcend to somewhere else more meaningful.

From that point of the evening on, I was simply content to sit back with a magnanimous smile on my face and thoroughly enjoy every facet of the breathtaking café crowd. Jan's wife "Little Eva" (Anna's pet name for her because she of her petite frame) soon joined us. I saw how Anna valued her friendship as they chatted in Swedish. I ordered beers and slowly we drank and shared a few English words spoken now and then. The waitress, another beauty, asked for the order in Swedish. She soon brought salads and open-faced shrimp sandwiches on white porcelain plates. The sounds of the bar nearby muffled the taps on the china, as they discussed (I guessed) where we must go next.

Gothenburg is an industrialized city. Shipbuilders, car manufacturers and Scandinavian architecture border a vast harbor resplendent with the sights and sounds only modern cities could provide. A canal system runs through the center of the city, carrying boats throughout the country and reminding all of its Nordic past.

We strolled from The Palace down The Avenue—the main street of activity, full of people in shops and bars. The sun, shining, had called forth Gothenburg's youth, all of whom were dressed down to ensure tan lines, which had been postponed by this region's dark and cold winters.

The city life was in stark contrast to its outer shorelines, dotted with large rock outcroppings, and its suburbs, densely packed with red- and yellow-painted houses overlooking bleak shores and boat docks. At night, there was no missing the multitude of sailboats moored next to seaside restaurants and bars, all of which were packed with waterproofed sailors and well-dressed regulars.

One of our obligations on this trip was to attend several birthday parties. Our first celebration was right after lunch and was for our nephew, Magnus Brändstöm, Anna's sister Maria's son.

Magnus lived in a small, three-room apartment that overlooked a courtyard full of activity. Bicycles were locked up under shade trees; boulders protruded from pavers, which provided a place to sit in the afternoon shade. I was really looking forward to seeing Adam and Olivia, who were meeting us at Magnus's party. Our reuniting was everything I hoped, as they greeted me with a flurry of questions, most of which were to reassure me that I had been missed.

Eva Nilsson, Anna's other sister, soon arrived with their mother, Siv, and greeted me with one of her warm, wet kisses. The party soon filled the small apartment to capacity. We needed more space, so we moved it to Siv's, not far, where I finally settled in with the transfer of luggage, which contained an old whiskey to break the ice. We sat outside at a table with a brightly-colored tablecloth situated under a yellow canopy and awaited Jan's arrival. This was, indeed, a full clan gathering—my entire family, plus the sisters, their husbands, Little Eva, and Siv, as well as some of my nieces and nephews. We made quite the gathering—boisterous and jovial.

A white van eventually pulled up, and I made my way to

its large window to see Jan for the first time since his stroke. Although he was in a wheelchair, he appeared happy to see me. The feeling was mutual. Jan could no longer work, could say only a few sounds, new words he'd made up, but we knew he was there inside. His joys and anger were expressed in his eyes, expressions, and in the frustration of some of his movements. He'd taken up painting, and his art was quite good—simple impressions, bright colors, but it was hard to believe how he'd lost so much at fifty-five years of age. Why does shit like this happen to good people?

Friday night in Gothenburg equated a salmon dinner, which Siv had prepared to perfection. As we all sat around eating and drinking, it dawned on me that this would be the modus operandi for our stay.

A short night's rest later, our day began with breakfast and strong coffee. Anna and the girls wanted to go shopping, so we went over to Little Eva's house. Doing my best to gather up support, I suggested we lunch at The Palace once again. Afterwards, Adam and I had no intention of shopping with the ladies, so I turned to him and said, "Let the girls go do their thing. We'll go have a beer."

Ah, yes, my young son was growing up fast.

We hit an old bar, and I ordered the drafts. The bartender pulled out two cold mugs, placed them under a tall Carlsbad tap handle and filled them at an angle—clearly taking pride in his profession. We retired outside, slowly enjoying our hops, as Adam filled me in on his adventures.

"We landed in Stockholm, and Mom got a stick shift car. And on our way to Uggelboda we saw moose." It had taken them four hours to get back to the place that Adam had been baptized seventeen years earlier. "We drove on dirt roads looking at a lot of nature. My cousins took me around to meet everyone, so I'd reach out my hand to those Swedes saying, 'Hello,' then I'd wait just a second and say, 'America.'"

"That must have worked well," I replied. He showed me the action. I was so happy he was having the time of his life.

"The internet is a pain in the ass. I have to go find wireless hotspots in neighbors' yards to e-mail Stephanie, they don't have good e-mail here. Eric took me to the air force base, and I got to wear this helmet and flight suit, sit in the pilot seat," he said as he took a deep gulp.

He had so much to say, to tell me—he was so excited that it seemed like he jumped from one thing to another. He downloaded everything as fast as he could, and I could barely get a word in. "There are so many beautiful girls here too. It's great having this beer, thanks Pops."

"Skol," I said, as I lifted the glass, knowing even then that moments like these were fleeting.

We sat, talked some more about the people walking by and the bikers in leather at the table in the corner, while we had our rite of passage, where a father and son shared their first beer. We both reveled in the moment—it was a mix of pride and just cool, like Steve McQueen having a drink with Johnny Depp.

Once we finished our beers, we walked down to the harbor and stepped aboard a ship-like hotel. It had an outdoor restaurant on its main deck, and we sat contentedly, no need to say much. We were father and son, but we were also friends amid a crowd of young and beautiful women and eager men under the warm Swedish afternoon light.

Watching all the activity, Adam said, "See all these girls? They're everywhere in this town, but I love Stephanie, and she's my soul mate. I wish she was here."

From what I saw in his eyes and his heart, it was obvious Adam was deeply in love, and I was so happy, so proud for him to have found such passion and to know what that felt like at such a young age.

But we didn't have a great deal of time right then to continue that conversation, although I wanted to. We'd been asked to attend every family gathering in Gothenburg. These parties were continuous discussions in Swedish, until someone spoke English, which meant I was up. I'd answer, they'd politely answer back, then there'd be a sidebar in Swedish, and it went on like that until I'd get up, pausing it all. They'd stop, and I'd offer a whiskey, a sort of Swedish peace prize.

Our engagement that evening was Jan's daughter Julia's thirtieth birthday party. It started out pleasant enough, but I soon found myself defending the U.S. to young Swedish professionals—writers and socialists—who seem to have iron-willed, yet untraveled opinions. They lectured me about modern socialism, America's economic ignorance and how our war efforts were unjust. Soon enough they just marveled in their own seeming greatness, professing Sweden to be the new temple of evolution—even telling me that America's beacon of light was in the past. I loved Sweden—that's a fact. I loved America. There was room for all of us here at this table.

I should have provided the fitting epitaph for that moment. Instead, I joined the children outside, playing monkey-in-the-middle, some game with a ball that the players kept just out of reach from that dancing monkey, which I must say was more honest and blameless than those professionals inside.

Later, we drove to Siv's house with Little Eva and Magnus. Adam immediately got out his laptop and went straight to his wireless drop site—under a tree in front of one of Siv's neighbors' where he connected to the Internet for an e-mail chat with Stephanie. This was a ritual, done with his heart.

I watched from a distance, and then joined him. I couldn't help but smile as I saw him drift through cyberspace, his fingers clicking away at his keyboard—Stephanie's hands on the other end doing just the same

With one final dramatic tap, he sent his message to Stephanie.

The silence spanned several agonizing minutes for him, then his fingers were busily tapping away at the keyboard again.

His smile spoke volumes.

25 A Dinner

June–July, 2008

No matter how much time and distance you place between yourself and certain family members, sometimes there's no escaping the drama of marriage. When you don't see people for a long time, you think it'll all be hearts and flowers when you do, but then again, I've lived long enough to know that's not always the case.

As the conclusion of our visit to Gothenburg drew near, we had one last chance to make this a memorable occasion for Anna's sister, Eva, who deserved a special touch, since her marriage was all but washed-up. Although a stylish dinner seemed to be the perfect solution, our only obstacle was Eva's self-absorbed husband Bengt, who had to be included, if not completely occupy the center of attention, always at the expense of his wife. Eva, the most unselfish member of our extended family, was the epitome of gentleness and love, and her humble soul knew nothing but generosity—even to those who did not deserve her kindhearted affections.

Desiring a special place for the family feast, Anna chose a seaside restaurant in the suburb where Eva and Anna grew up. There were nine of us that night, and the location could not have been more beautiful. Our table was set with exquisite silver, crystal and china, and we had a perfect view of the rock-lined harbor with its sailboats always coming and going. I ordered white wine for the table; even got Adam a beer, my girls had Cokes. We enjoyed hors d'oeurves of escargot and salmon on toast—all meant to draw out the time for Anna, Eva and Siv.

It was a lovely evening on all counts, well almost all counts—simple talk; the adults slowly becoming intoxicated—except for Bengt's bizarre behavior when it came time to order the main course. In an effort to impress our waitress, Bengt started with small talk about the fish on the menu, and then he asked her about the weight of his soon-to-be-ordered fish.

"How many grams will the fish be?"—then something about what should be a proper serving weight, as if there were standards for such things. He kept talking to her, trying so hard to impress, as if she would grant him some sexual favor when he came back ten nights from now. We were all used to his pretentiousness. I just wanted to say to her, "He's a door-to-door vacuum cleaner salesman, maybe you need one?" She knew his type, must have put up with flirtatious, obnoxious chitchat before, since she was a goddess who, most likely, would someday arrive at newsstands on the cover of the Victoria Secret catalog.

Eva looked at him, as if to say, "Would you please just shut the fuck up?" but she didn't say a word, she just stared. I knew she was at the breaking point you have to get out of or be crushed. The waitress took the rest of our orders, no more insensitivity from Bengt, except his two piercing eyes. Bengt knew I was buying, so he ordered away; soup for himself, another bottle of wine, then a beer. I didn't care as long as he contained himself for the rest of the night. They cleared the appetizer plates, made sure the napkins were on laps, and two or three of the wait staff brought out the main courses. The table filled with smells of crab cakes, flounder, and the steak that Adam had ordered. There was white gravy on the side, next to the summer fresh greens, warm bread and whipped butter. The meal was exquisite: fish sautéed in butter; lightly salted, crisp vegetables; bittersweet wine; warm bread with melted butter. All this only a bit soured by the thought of the embarrassment Bengt caused his wife, which could not be softened with orders of desserts and coffees. Siv thought it excess, and it may have been, but the kids loved sweets. And I knew this crowd would never be back.

Eva's misery was obvious—having had him at her side for too long, listening to his intermittent rambling about fish weights, I guess. We were all aware that Eva needed our kindness, and that this pompous man who left the dinner table to have a cigarette, or possibly to carry on his discussion with the waitress, was no longer essential to Eva's life. Eva wanted to end her marriage, which pained all those who knew and cared about her. We all felt her desire for escape into an unknown happiness, into some place, some life without her vain husband anywhere to be found.

After one more round of iced Cokes, the kids ran off to take a look around. Shortly thereafter I went in search of them, leaving the three ladies alone.

In no time at all, I spotted the kids at the harbor, playing on the docks and adjacent rocks.

I thought back while watching them, about the last trip I took with my father to South Bend, Indiana. It was a family reunion. I took Hanna with me. James and Lynn made the trip too. Dad had bought all our plane tickets. There was this river where he rented a boat we all got in, except for Dad. He stayed behind on the bank, watching. The boat pitched and yawed as it ran down the river. Lynn and James were tossed out, while I held on to Hanna. My father kept watching as I yanked Lynn, then James back in. I often wonder what was on his mind as he looked on from the shore.

26 Road Trip to Copenhagen

June–July, 2008

I was eager to show the family a little of Copenhagen, plus revisit an old hotel where Anna and I stayed on our first trip to Europe twenty-five years earlier.

We packed some bags for the drive through the south of Sweden and across the new bridge between Malmo and Copenhagen. It was a pleasant drive, and along the way Anna noticed signs promoting the Swedish Open, a tennis tournament at the seaside resort town of Bastad. Because it was lunchtime, and we were all eager to see something new, we turned off the main road.

Signs picturing tennis players ran along the road leading to the small town, where its old church and graveyard stood in contrast to the tournament's red-clay courts, which were surrounded by a modern tennis center, and its nearby seaside restaurants. Set back from the beaches were unpretentious homes overflowing with flowered gardens.

As with all major tennis tournaments, the well-dressed were in attendance. Most of the men were sporting bright sweaters draped over Lacoste shirts, and there was no mistaking the women—their long, tanned legs jutting from beneath short, white skirts, complete with high heels. And the best place to admire this mix of Scandinavian beauty was at the tennis center hotel's dining area.

Of course, as our family of six grabbed a table for lunch, we became aware that we were an oddity. Our four children erupted into normal conversation, which elicited looks from everyone within earshot. After all, Swedish was the norm. Our outside table faced the sea. A slight breeze blew in from the west as everyone looked at everyone else to measure the importance and beauty of those around them.

Due to our sojourn to Bastad, we arrived late at Copenhagen's Admiral Hotel. We were given two split-level rooms on the sixth floor of this eighteenth-century waterfront hostel. Built of massive wooden beams and brick, the structure served as a grain-drying granary during the trading periods of the 1780s. It was several blocks from not only the King's Palace, but also the city's historic waterfront where old ships continued to dock next to outdoor cafés, and where sailors still drank hard and long amid the pleasant aromas of century-old wood and freshly caught seafood.

Sadly, our Danish stay was for only thirty-six hours. We made the most of it by strolling along the streets and peering through shop windows. The kids were having a good time, eyes fixed on boat-lined channels, landscaped with outdoor tables where smells and sights brought out their hunger, which was never very far away. They wanted to know where we were going to eat. We walked down a narrow, stony road to a courtyard where waiters passed under brightly colored umbrellas. Small children danced to a musician playing his violin. We got a shaded table, and the maître d', knowing we were tourists, had the waiter bring English menus. We ordered, it was late, but that was when the locals dined, so we felt the city's life, while we watched the expressions and heard the string of foreign chatter.

Exhausted from our long day, we wanted to turn in early, but Olivia insisted on a bicycle ride, and she was going to make sure it was arranged. Always the precise planner, I took her down to the lobby where she approached the desk, barely able to see over it, asking, "Can I get six bikes from you tomorrow morning? My family wants to go on a bike ride."

The concierge saw I was watching, and she went along with the little charade.

"Can I get your room number? I will need your name."

She handed her the key, "My name is Olivia Stephens."

"What time would you need them?"

"In the morning, after breakfast,"

"We have six bikes for 10:00 A.M., Okay?"

"Thank you, my dad will pay for them."

The blonde lady at the front desk returned the key to Olivia, saying, "See you tomorrow."

And so we rode along the waterfront that morning, visiting the King's Palace and his ever-vigilant guards; we watched the changing of the guard, paused at the sculpture of The Little Mermaid, where swarms of day-trippers were taking her picture. We continued our two-wheeled journey to an old fort embankment where fearsome cannons pointed to Swedish shores. Beneath high clouds, Adam raced ahead, using his mysterious compass, similar to the kind that returning salmon have in them, leading us with self-confidence, the kind that you grow into. He led us over a drawbridge and back along the sea road that took us directly back to the Admiral Hotel. Olivia was so pleased that she had pulled off this summer adventure. The trip was much-needed exercise, mixed with laughs under the glitter of midmorning. At that moment I saw Olivia feeling pride, and I was proud of her too!

Bags packed, Adam and I loaded the car, and we all drove up a grassed and flowered coastline, the seashore dotted with hotels and restaurants. We drove along the coast road, and the wind rushed over the Danish flags dotting the roadside, as the signs gave us the kilometers to Helsingør. We parked the car, had hours to kill before the last ferry to Sweden, so we walked along the ancient stone streets of the port city. Olivia saw one of her cousin Julia's writer friends eating ice cream, who we had met a few days earlier at Julia's birthday party.

Excited to see a familiar face sitting with friends at a nearby table, I extended a most-gracious: "Hello, we met at Julia's. What a small world it is to see you here."

Unfortunately, the warmth was not reciprocated. It was as if these Swedes were upset with our American invasions. They remained aloof, making me feel unwelcomed and unwanted, so we quickly departed. It was clear that the war in Iraq and the economic downturn somehow spoke for each American, and we all felt it without saying a word.

Enough with the Danes and the holiday Swedes—I wasn't going to let that moment color the rest of our trip. We drove onto a double-ended ferry that would take us back to Sweden. The ferry ride reminded me of the kind of boat travels I've read about in novels—the sea breeze brushing against our faces and blowing our hair back as crests of small waves broke off the boat's bow, but then we docked into a ferry slip, drove over the metal ramp, each pair of tires causing it to clang, through the passport checkpoint, around the city of Helsingborg, towards Anna's summer home, Uggelboda.

27 Uggelboda's Lake Hjälmaren

June–July, 2008

Sitting in a dew-damp chair on the shore in the early morning calm, there was an occasional splash, and ripples expanded and dissipated as small fish broke the surface. And I remember thinking, this country, all splash and ripple—all water and beauty. So much sea, but when I felt truly peaceful in Sweden, it was always near water, and then I realized, thinking back to our trips to Mississippi, home at Providence Lake, to those rivers and waterfalls of the Yosemite, that it was always near water where I found peace, just as there at Lake Hjälmaren, my peace was in its sounds, the taste on my lips, its shock on my skin when I stepped into that icy lake to bathe, knowing that water was used to baptize my children.

At Lake Hjälmaren, old boats sat beneath trees, surrounded by grass—landlocked, but thirsty to hit the water, to glide its freedom, to ferry someone somewhere, to be useful. I realized that even boats need the water to be fulfilled—their duty is clear. Rock-lined shores with delicate purple-and-yellow flowers poked through the heavy moss. The morning air was cool and damp; the water's placid gray surface brightened as sunlight came through the clouds to light the moss-covered boulders which protruded above the lake's surface.

Floating in the distance were green, tree-covered islands that seemed to roll and meld with the sky above. A bird swooped down—its gray feathers, white head and black beak mirrored in the lake's surface as it glided away with a worm to its nest of babies.

The sun, having broken through in the distance, lit emerald-green meadows with massive pines seeming to just skim the sky. I remember the light changed there so quickly—its shifting patterns turning grays to blues, and blues to silvergreen; the light's diffusion through limbs and leaves provided the transparent shades of greens throughout the morning.

That lake was where families went to do simple things, to see people with names such as Siv, Ulla, Erik, Valdemar, Maria, Linnea, Klas, Jan, Anna and Eva. They worked in kitchens and talked through open windows, swam in the ice-cold waters abundant with fish.

During the quiet mornings and midsummer nights, it was impossible not to feel lazy. Each day started with hand-cut, homemade bread and creamy sliced cheese, all washed down with strong coffee—all simple. I wanted to take the simplicity home with me—pack it up in a suitcase and smuggle it on the plane somehow.

We gathered around tables filled with Swedish chatter and conversations, which, other than "good morning," I did not understand. Here plans were made and forgotten, dinners were discussed and re-discussed, all in the shadows of clouds moving lazily high above. Life was: Flowers blooming, a warm sun radiating against your skin, and finding yourself drifting off to sleep while reclining in a wooden chair.

Here, time was drawn out. Old people were entitled; the elder voices of Siv and Ulla were not only listened to, but also deeply respected. People said, "I am glad you are here" in one breath, yet gossiped as only small-town folks can. They also babbled about old times for hours. Stories were repeated for the benefit of the young, while being carved and turned like wood spindles on old lathes. Each person added his or her voice, or told their own stories—which were sometimes listened to, sometimes not.

Maria, Anna's sister, read her book upside down, while instructing Anna on something irrelevant. The talk seemed endless. Not only did everyone have something to say, they also had no trouble saying it. I recalled, there in that place, surrounded by my wife's family, my father telling me, "A shared concern is half a concern." God, that was a good line, why did he not have more sayings like that? Why did he not practice what he said? Then, right in front of me I saw it in my brother-in-law, in how he commanded his fishing boat and expeditions on the water, something my father could never master, nor enjoy.

Maria sat at an outside table, her hair, usually neatly trimmed, was out of place, and her voice had this authority which matched the expression on her face, which big sisters have. She said to Anna in her broken English, "Listen here, you must listen to me, wake up your children, they can't sleep all the day. They need something nice to eat before we leave for shopping." As the older sister, Maria felt the need to direct Anna often. Maria's husband Erik sat and admired his wife's steady outspoken flow of suggestions.

Between meals, reading and sunning, we soon settled into the routine of the day: A trip to town to get supplies; a little tennis at the well-maintained red-clay courts, where Swedish boys practiced their skills; a swim in the tideless, frigid waters that woke every cell in my body; a card- or board- game, or a walk to the café for coffee and ice cream.

Contentment is family. Anna was reclined on the couch with her mother, uncomfortable, yet relaxed and untroubled. Siv was in her nineties, always stylish, not a grey hair on her head, running around with a well-meaning look on her face, wanting to be helpful. Although Siv's fragile, arthritic body was pressed to the inside of the couch, Anna held her hand, her body hanging slightly off the couch's edge. They sat in silence until discomfort required one of them to move, which was usually toward the kitchen for food. Siv belonged there, and it was impossible to envision Uggelboda without her flying around.

Fishing was a serious matter. Poles were cast, traps dropped, and nets set along prime nocturnal routes. Of course, each fishing procedure was defined by varying levels of personal experience, which I had little of. The nets must be checked for fish, so Maria enlisted Olivia and me as the crew for Captain Erik and his small, white rowboat that was moored on a slightly submerged timber boat-rack and secured with a cable connected to a beech tree. Erik instructed Olivia to put in the drain plug. She must have received training in the two weeks before I arrived, or she would not have been entrusted with such a responsibility. The cable was extended, and the captain and Olivia boarded the boat. It was my job to launch the craft.

But no sooner did I complete this task, than I was promoted—rowing to Erik's commands. It was soon apparent from the concern etched onto Erik's face that my rowing skills were not up to his standards. I had no history of rowing, but, after all, it was only rowing, how hard could that be? Why was he taking it so seriously? I guessed he needed to correct me, just like Maria corrected Anna. Although little was said, he kept my directional shortcomings to a minimum by occasionally pointing toward the nets' buoys.

Upon reaching the outermost buoy, Captain Erik barked out his orders: "Stop here. Row the boat stern towards the nets and then backwards diagonally. No, not like that. Okay, that's a little better."

Erik was a lifetime military man accustomed to giving and receiving orders, which he did with a military voice. He spoke often in orders. As he lifted the nets, he carefully placed them on netting tackle. Once we pulled up the first fish of the day, Eric was emphatic in his instruction, "Stop immediately, please," as he reviewed the fish for size and species. Erik gave special attention to its removal from the net, but I was not sure if this was for the sake of the fish or if it was the net that concerned him.

Erik returned the smaller fish to the lake, tossing them back with such force and voracity that it will remind them to never again be so careless.

Upon our return to the shore, we disembarked, and under the all-vigilant eye of Captain Erik, we tied the boat to the tree. Olivia removed the drain plug, then Erik, Olivia and I heaved the fish onto dry ground—the last time they'll see dry ground again. When I inquired about the possibility of a fine fish dinner, I was told the day's catch would be prepared for a future meal. Erik mumbled something or other about "being broiled at home."

The morning turned to afternoon wind and summer rain. Much to everyone's relief, the rain quickly came and went. After all, sun and fresh air had been a long time in arriving. Putting aside memories of a long and brutal winter, the noon sun brought everyone outdoors to enjoy the warmth with a nature-walk or merely to join friends or family at the local outdoor café for coffee and conversation amid crisp air and a light breeze.

Afternoons in Uggelboda seemed endless. Time moved slowly, and any worries I had were forgotten as the days lazily rolled along.

At the time for an afternoon bath, Sofia, Olivia, Anna, and I eased into the water. Its refreshing chill was somewhat tempered by the sun, but what really warmed us was swimming. It was a pleasant experience, indeed. After a while, it didn't seem that cold.

Adam and Hanna were nowhere to be found. I found Hanna still in bed reading; Adam soon appeared walking down the grass incline, hair all messed up, same clothes he left in the night before, looking as if he has been up all night. His aunt and mother seemed proud of him, grins across their faces, and it seemed as though they were recalling their past all-nighters, and there was no shame in those smiles. I tempered my response. "How was it, up all night? Lots of girls at the party?" I concealed my jealousy, as I recalled the first night with his mother walking naked from the water. I did my best to not condone Adam's Swedish summer of fun in front of the girls. Of course, Hanna measured my response, looking to see if there was anger brimming. There certainly was none in Olivia's and Sofia's smiles at their brother. They seemed to relish in Adam's ability to test my parenting capacities.

We took naps, made trips to Vingåker, the local one-store town, where we bought our groceries; we inspected nets, consumed candy, and everyone settled in toward the evening. Sofia and Olivia had picked strawberries for me to taste. They were small, but so full of flavor for something so little.

Erik was in the kitchen, preparing dinner, which would be served at seven on the dot. He seemed to enjoy his role as chef. We rearranged the table, making sure all of us could be seated around it.

There were twelve of us that night, each arriving at his or her own pace; all dressed a little special for the evening's affairs. Erik had prepared a feast topped with sliced lemons that were to be squeezed onto the shrimp. We filled plates and took seats as the evening became unruffled with spirits and fine food. Once the kids finished their meals and left the table to go explore and play outside, the rest of us consumed plate after plate of shrimp and glasses of beer.

We surrendered to a pleasant evening of light-hearted conversations about past trips together, when Swedes came to San Diego, New York and now to Georgia. This brought on playful stories of our time together in places like deserts—something the Swedes can only imagine from pictures in books—to drives along California's Highway 1 coastline, to the skyscrapers and secret places found within the streets of New York, then to our home in the tall pines of Georgia. There was a round of drunken proposals for future trips—trips which would not be made or plans for even remembered in the morning

It was at this dinner that we needed an historic clarification of a trip made to Yosemite many years earlier, around 1993, by Anna, Adam and me, which sparked our need to relive it. This invoked the procurement of boxes of carefully marked slides and an old rotary projector. We drew the curtains, made a screen on a wall and poured whiskeys all around. As the evening passed, we queued up slide upon slide from our trips and drank more whiskey.

As the dim evening light marched on, we tired as the last slide of some boat on a river with someone, who no one recognized, manning it clicked by. And with that, the carousel clicked one last time and our cups ran dry. Only a few of us men were left to have one final drink over a discussion of U. S. politics, which I wanted nothing to do with.

The night ended with no one sober, yet all well-sedated against an early-morning light that would soon shine through the cracks of our window drapes.

28 Hanna & Her Swedish Boys

June–July, 2008

We had every intention of getting in a few games of tennis during our time abroad. I'd lugged the rackets half-way across the world, and I was determined to make use of them—to get everyone out for a good sweat. Hanna seemed to be really looking forward to it.

In front of Vingåker's Säfstaholm Manor was a large pond with a streaming fountain that spit out Matisse paper-cut-outs, but in water. Shade trees hung along its borders, and across the way were two red-clay courts and a tennis barn with an indoor hard court. I'd known about these courts for years, drove by them before but had never played on them. Now it was time to step out onto the clay.

Adam wasn't quite interested. Just another court to him, so he sat in the car while Hanna and I inspected the red clay.

And wouldn't you know it, two young, blonde, Swedish boys, about Hanna's age, mid-teens, were out there playing, both at their baselines recovering each other's well-placed shots. It was obvious they had some skills in the game, and they moved with practiced grace, setting up their strokes with precision.

As Hanna and I walked onto the court, the boys glanced

our way for just the briefest of moments. Only later, on the drive back to Uggelboda, did I see that special gleam in Hanna's eyes. It only took one look to see that this trip had been an important one for Hanna—a pivotal moment in her life. There was a change in her face, in the way she smiled. Hanna had suddenly morphed into a young lady.

She was fifteen at that point and modest, strong-willed and had a youthful beauty that was in stark contrast to her tomboy childhood, which she earned with her rough and tumble exchanges with Adam. She liked to be listened to, but when ignored, her sarcastic humor cut deep. Her seemingly impenetrable outer shell could be broken, but only when she allowed you past her well thought-out emotions. And although I knew she loved me dearly, I was often on the receiving end of her many cynical critiques—critiques which she often hurled at her brother and sisters as well.

But, right then, at that moment, I knew she wanted to play tennis, and I was anxious for a father–daughter showdown as well. So, we went back to the house and pulled on our sneakers and headed to the courts, rackets in hand, while Adam stayed behind.

Of course, the two Swedish boys were still there. I couldn't get them to play a set with Hanna and me. Both times I asked, they politely declined in perfect English and went on about their game. But after our quick warm-up, they were convinced, and we were soon playing a game of doubles. They held serve, we held serve. The ball moved slower than Hanna and I were used to since we played mostly on the fast hard-courts back home. The boys picked on me, had me running all over, wanted to be in good grace with Hanna, I guessed. There were lots of good shots, and Hanna handled herself well, not letting the boys' power push her around. We played a respectable set but lost, 6–3. That was not my intention, but it worked out nicely when I said to them, "Okay, one of you gets Hanna now."

She looked at me, her eyes full of surprise, not quite sure of herself, but pleased with my suggestion. She strolled over to the younger of the two, a tall and strong fourteen-year-old—one of those strapping Viking-types her mother had so often spoke of. And as the elder boy tried to hide his dejection over being stuck with me, all I could think of was: So, this is how it is. Daughters move on, but hopefully come back to their Pops, somehow she will need me. I thought of how my sister Lynn needed my father to rescue her. I knew Hanna was strong-willed, and at some point, innocence does pass into that budding interest in what's opposite.

Hanna's partner wanted to impress her with his skills. After every good shot, his or hers, he offered her a high-five. Soon she was responding in kind. And whenever he said, "Come on, Hanna," she smiled at the sound of his voice. And sometimes she even looked across to me.

Admittedly, that was a peculiar moment for a father. On one hand, there was no joy in seeing your daughter's heart stolen by another; on the other hand, I was so happy to see the uncertain bewilderment and pleasure in Hanna's face. By seven we had to leave for dinner, but I asked the boys; "How about another match tomorrow?" "Yes, that would be fine," and one of them ran off to check court schedules.

"Let's play at 11:00, does that work for you?" I looked at Hanna. She was excited, so all I could say was, "See you tomorrow."

Of course, that moment couldn't arrive soon enough for Hanna. And when it did, we were greeted by rain. She kept insisting to me that our newfound friends would still show up to play.

About an hour before the match, I heard her asking her mother in a pleading tone, "Where's my hair straightener?" Shortly thereafter, my no-longer-so-little-girl appeared in a recently cleaned tennis outfit, hair pulled to the side in a half-ponytail, looking more eager than usual.

"Let's go," she said, holding her racket under her arm as if she were off to play a Davis Cup match. I'd never seen her so excited about the game before.

We arrived early. The boys soon pulled up with their father, who they said had a big serve; an elder brother had also tagged along. All seemed pleased to meet Hanna and me, while confirming their young son's evening stories of foreigners in Vingåker. They stayed to watch our match for a while, much to the delight of the youngest son, who took up right where he left off—giving his high-fives and embracing Hanna's smiles. We would not see them again, but Hanna did get his e-mail address.

29 Stockholm

June–July, 2008

Adam, Hanna and I boarded the train from Vingåker, while Sofia, Olivia and Anna drove since there was not enough room in the rental car for us and the luggage. Arriving first at the hotel, Hanna started her cynical objections, "Not close enough to the action, the rooms are out-dated, the hallway feels like prison, Mom's not going to like this." That was a bomb that I couldn't let go off…knowing upon her mother's arrival I would have a full-blown fiasco on my hands since the girls and Anna were known to work together when they need-ed to better their accommodations or select a restaurant more to their liking. I knew it too. The hotel looked so much better on the Internet than it actually was, so I called the web service we'd booked through, and they said "You're stuck tonight, but tomorrow we put you at the Hilton. It borders the old town of Gala Stan." Our check-in was at noon, And with an apology, it was as simple as that. The place sucked, it was my fault. I had to correct it—that was my job, fixing messes.

How right Hanna was.

After Anna's initial onslaught on its location, not to men-tion how inconvenient the subway rides to dinners, museums, and parks would be, we changed hotels in the morning no questions asked. We took rooms at the Hilton—facing the sea, a channel and a lock station, just a bridge over to Gamla Stan, Stockholm's old town. Just outside our windows, we could see its church steeples, the City Hall where Nobel Prize minds met, and the burnt orange buildings of the island neighborhoods reflecting off blue waterways connected by water-taxi and bridges.

We were soon walking along ancient stone walkways to shops, cafés next to Stockholm's National Cathedral and Royal Palace, and then on to the site where the Nobel Prizes were awarded. Stockholm was a spectacular old city—a city of islands connected by ferries that took us to parks, museums, grand hotels and Nobel halls. Or, better yet, out to the archipelagos, the island outcroppings so resplendent that only a divine hand could have created them.

We spent one day cruising among these archipelagos in an old steamboat, enjoying its outdoor decks, dining rooms and lounge chairs as time slowly passed us by. The only thing that was more enjoyable than sea air was the salmon and meatballs we dined on. Then it was off to sleep in some deck chair or simply looking at Sweden's natural beauty. That way of life was new to our children, new to me in many ways, it was a sudden understanding of what was important: The ones you're with, those you celebrate with at tables. There occurrences struck me, in words like, "Please pass me the bread"; "This place is so nice"; "Would you like some more wine?"; or "Look at that dog trying to steal your hotdog." It didn't really matter what they said, it was being there to hear it, to say it because time is so short in places like that.

It was breathtaking to navigate the very waterways Vikings once traveled en route to invading Russia. Now, the island communities were dotted with quaint summer homes—yellow and red and blue—all positioned under clear skies and accessible only by boat.

We were soon moored at one of the island towns, and we disembarked to walk up and down its one main street. The journey took no time at all. We came across a 1958 BMW motorcycle, its black gas tank labeled proudly with an historical stainless-steel plate, date stamped onto it. The cycle was parked on the cobblestone street next to an art gallery—the bike's uncomplicated design fit right in with the forgotten way of life that was present on this island.

An old fort sat isolated, one-hundred yards away at sea. If a tourist was so inclined, a boat went back and forth to the fort, no one went but me.

We found a table at an outdoor café, resting in the shade under its umbrella, partaking in a few beers and an informal meal. We watched the community's citizens and fellow travelers come and go, but mostly we were content viewing boats—sail, steam and those with motors—as they lazily skirted about the waterway.

Such was life in an archipelago.

When a summer drizzle began, an old woman and her grandchild scurried for cover. They huddled right next to us, just under the awning, not saying a thing. We understood they needed the dry patch, as they watched each other and the rain that came down. But then, in a matter of minutes, the rain disappeared and out came the sun again. No one seemed too concerned—life goes on.

Our steamboat was on the horizon, making its return. Compared to the sailboats and motorboats moving rapidly past it, the steamboat was outdated. But, in reality, it was a vessel of vast distinction—its narrow metal hull painted white and crowned with a black smokestack ringed with yellow bands.

As a trailing plume of steam drifted above the boat's stern and was carried into a windless, blue sky, I couldn't help but think that the captain felt great pride as his vessel moved along with a grace reserved for antiquity.

30 The Vasa of 1628

June–July, 2008

Inside a vast wooden structure on the banks of Stockholm's harbor, there was a vessel of war laying at rest. In 1628, the Vasa set sail from Stockholm's harbor, traveled less than a nautical mile and sank. And there it remained, encased in the mud of the frigid and unpolluted harbor, for more than three centuries.

I could have found myself in a spot like that, creating questions that couldn't be answered right now. I had inherited a history that I did not want to pass along, and I overcompensated for what my father did not do or give to make sure my children knew I was always around, if only to watch them play well into the night or to take them somewhere or another. More than once old attitudes surfaced—I could have settled the arguments better, listened more, ignored less, but as time passed, I gave up more and more of that history so we could tell new stories some day and put away the old ones, like I am doing now.

It was in my childhood when Captain Paul Stephens made his maiden voyage. My brother, sister and I in tow, he set sail from San Diego Harbor to forget the type of transgressions you discover pollute all those holy things in yourself. His discovery came as his wife poured out his life in a fury that flowed like a calamity, where he was losing hold of dreams, losing, it felt like, late in the game. For my father, those sailboats were the escape to an unknown, which provided him pleasant memories, and they were for us too. When it was calm, so nice to be out there, the wind blowing us along, pulling the ropes, and when the sails flopped to a new direction, it took us with them. The salt mist sprayed in your face; small ripples reflected the light like stars in the water. If only it could have lasted, our happiness withered too quickly.

The water was a sanctuary where he meant well, but he did not recognize we were frightened on those over-winded days; still, he'd pack us into the family car and head for the marina, where we'd join this most ancient of mariners struggling on the seas.

Trouble was, my father had no earthly idea what he was doing.

Leaving the calm waters close to shore, the gentle splashes against the fiberglass hull were short-lived. Once the wind took hold of the sails in deep water, our fear grew in proportion to Dad's inept skills as a sailor. Despite us kids taking refuge in the barren hull—with nothing to cling to except our panic and each other—our father had escaped his worries that he'd left back home, and we all helped by conceding.

As the force of the cascading waves slapped against the hull, the power of those blows were buffeted only by our life vests. In essence, we were scared to death, fully realizing that the only thing standing between us and an unforgiving sea was our father. Not a comforting thought.

I could envision all of us floating along, only to be saved by the orange tied-on pillows and the coast guard's boat.

All the while, our captain braced the wind with grim determination and unblinking eyes locked on a distant horizon, nautical miles separated him from a husband's worst nightmare—a drunken, unfaithful wife.

Much to his credit, Dad always managed to get us safely back to port. He never sank the boat, and he did, it seemed, find some solitude, some peace in the adventures, sustaining himself for what was to come—conscious or unconscious of all that lay before us, I do not know. But there was something truthful and sublime in it for him, and I recognize something similiar in myself and my relationship with Adam and his tennis.

But not for my family, as we all gazed in amazement upon the partially restored vessel—reflecting on its dark-brown color, almost like walnut or cherry that had been polished time and time again—there was little wonder why it never joined the Swedish fleet at sea. It was August 10, 1628; the Vasa was on her maiden voyage, Captain Hansson at the helm. Light breeze that day, the ship's gun ports were open, set to fire a salute. A strong gust of wind hit her, causing her to heel quickly to port. The next gust finished her, and seawater poured into the open ports, pulling her under, only 140 yards from shore. All that remained visible for King Gustavus, Adolphus the Great, and his court was her main and fore masts. The largest and mightiest ship of its day, the Vasa was too tall at the stern, thus rendering it much too top-heavy.

What failed to sustain Sweden's military might more than 382 years ago was a living testimonial not only to this country's storied past, but also to its capacity to endure after total failure.

As I looked up from behind the ship, which was protected now against the ravages of deterioration within a climate-controlled building, I could not help but admire the craftsmanship, five-hundred sculptures of all types: Angels, devils, gods, and lions decorated the stern castle and gun decks, telling the artist's stories in carving. Such ornamentation rendered the ship more of a work of art than a vessel of war, which seems fitting—a modern sculpture of such a peaceful nation.

In a moment of reflection, I watched as boat after boat, with actual captains, navigated across the bay and tied up to the dock where the Vasa set sail. Tourists disembarked to tread on history where all the citizenry of Stockholm once came to watch as their king's magnificent ship launched and subsequently sank—supposedly a prized possession, no more.

Ironically, due to an almost unbelievable recovery and

restoration effort by Sweden, the Vasa stands even taller—a haunting reminder, for the people of Sweden and us tourists, of the folly of war. The boat's obituary says only nice things about it. Its secrets were left on the bottom of the sea, a long time ago.

31 A Day with Sofia

July, 2008

It was the end of July 2008, and the days started late in our Stockholm hotel. Anna and I bathed, and our children slept in. There were two rooms, two morning schedules—both the same, yet both different.

I found an old bakery just minutes over the bridge; it had fresh apple strudel covered with vanilla cream. The baker prepared warm pastry each day, and there were china cups and saucers stacked carefully next to a coffee server, where drips from its spout landed onto a silver bowl stained from years of use.

A blue porcelain sugar bowl and creamer were next to a silver-plated server, its scuffs mark its age. The set sat on a wooden table in the center of the room facing a painting of an old Swedish king. The table was covered with ironed linen, its creases folded perfectly at the corners. The patio held tables, which were always occupied, even though they were never quite level because of the uneven stones they sat on.

I came here every day with one of the kids or Anna, anyone willing to escape the comfort of their beds. Sofia and Olivia always asked, "Where are you going?"

I'd announce, "Meet me at the café." Their response was, "Bring back some bagels."

That was how my week of days in Stockholm began.

On one particular day, however, Sofia was graceful enough to share her time with just me. Usually, there was much hesitation in her decision-making—vacillation about shopping, roaming or partaking in my unheeded suggestions that we check out some particular piece of architecture or art museum. But that day it was obvious to me that Sofia didn't want to be a shopper or a roamer. I was heartened and stunned to understand that she was saying in her own way, "I just want to be with you, Papa."

She communicated with a mere look, like she always did—a look that said that that day was reserved for just her and me, father and daughter negotiating compromises and discovering interests, which, in turn, would connect us for hours, days and, hopefully, for the rest of our lives. It felt so necessary to grow these relationships over the nothing that we talked, walking together, smelling the cigarettes that were salted by the sea, listening to kids playing, as the sun fell outside.

Whatever she was thinking, I was grateful to be spending the morning and more with my ten-year-old child, my little Sofia.

So, off we went, hand-in-hand, her discussing with pride the knowledge she'd acquired in such a short time. Both of us had an interest in architecture, but that day's sojourn began at a Moderna Museet, over a bridge to the island of Skeppsholme. We viewed what others believe to be art. As we toured the main exhibit, it inspired a mutual feeling of dislike and disgust—paintings of human butchery and death. It was too much for such a young mind: Splashes of reds against human flesh, heads guillotined in baskets; the curator had hung the carnage and bloodbaths on his white walls.

Sofia said with urgency: "Dad, can we just get out of here? I don't like this at all."

And it felt like real killing. We headed for the nearest door in a hurry to escape. Any amount of time we'd spent there was too much. Ice cream seemed like a better plan, so I followed Sofia in her hunt.

We walked over a steel bridge crowned with the king's golden headdress, a reminder of his past glory and this royal capital city. His castle was just across the river from the National Gallery.

After ice cream we headed for an exhibition featuring the history of clocks—old Swedish and Swiss gold clocks, cuckoo and grandfather clocks ticking away in fractured harmony, running with a precision known only by those craftsmen who painstakingly toiled in their making.

It was dark and cool inside the exhibition hall, the individual rooms of which were shrouded by a stillness, dim lights casting shadows on the clocks as if they were second hands sweeping across time. Sofia was captivated by the exhibit; she walked off by herself to carefully examine her favorite clocks, inspecting a cuckoo or two. It was all about time in that room, my time with Sofia, how little time Anna and I had between their births and when they went off to college. That year felt so good being with them so much. I didn't know why I was doing it with such vigor, it just happened that way. Maybe I saw it as a way of putting my childhood desires behind me, but probably not, it was more like taking them to Anna's childhood from another time, where we could all still learn together.

On the floor above, we gazed at paintings of a past Swedish king; one in particular depicted him being carried off the field of battle, killed, according to tradition, by a bullet wound to his back. His white horse galloped before the troops with empty saddle stained with blood.

Rembrandts, Picassos, and Matisses—all painters who she'd ignored before—she now appreciated. She carried with her a small chair, provided by the museum, which she set up in front of the Rembrandts and some quaint nudes.

I had been luxuriating in an abundance of beer and food for a month now—four golden and scarlet weeks—an entire summer.

But now it was time to leave our Swedish summer and turn our thoughts to home. While this had been a proud moment, the connecting with Anna's family, seeing this part of the world, every page new, being able to extend a sense of family on such an exotic vacation, I knew the kids were home-sick—Adam, in particular, was eager to return to the arms of his Stephanie, the love of his life.

Before we departed, however, I made one last stop at my café for morning coffee. I was alone this time; the rest of the family remained in bed. But I headed back to the hotel with breakfast for all of them under my arm.

We ate, we packed, and then it was off to the airport in the car and a cab. We were not only running late, but also had too many bags. As Anna rushed off to return our rental car, I noticed that we were not the only travelers rushing to make their flight on time. Two tall men and a youthful woman, all carrying bright orange tennis bags, were second-to-last in line. We were, of course, last.

While we all barely boarded the plane in time, it turned out that one of gentlemen with tennis gear was Robin Söder-ling, Sweden's number one tennis player. In fact, his picture adorned the cover of the magazine I was carrying. As an added touch to the perfect vacation, Söderling autographed the mag-azine for Sofia once we were aboard the plane.

Thousands of air miles later, we arrived home late in the evening to find Flacken crying for our attention. Oliver ran to Sofia first, then to each of us—his way of confirming that the entire family was reunited. Adam had called Stephanie, and she was on her way over. The girls ran to their rooms, not tak-ing one single bag; they saw that as my job, and I had no idea why. It felt good to be home because, somehow, it had got-ten old after awhile to be in a place we knew was temporary. Those hotel rooms had been nice. It felt so good to go, but the return had more meaning since we no longer lived within a PO Box.

32 Gulf Islands & Fort Massachusetts

August 7, 2008

We had been home for two weeks from Sweden; it was a summer of heat and a year of being together more so than any other year. I knew this was my last chance for a family escape since I was making a business trip to Africa in two weeks. After that ALTA's fall tennis season would get underway. Adam and I were on that team together for the first time. I had waited ten years to play with my soon-to-be eighteen-year-old son. He was such a good player, and I was so excited to watch him flex his tennis muscles on the court against some pretty fierce and seasoned competitors. We were both looking forward to that.

School would start soon, and Anna voiced her desire to see the Morans and their kids, dog and party house before she had to start her scheduled driving to three schools, tennis and whatever other afterschool places. So we loaded the car, and the family, plus Oliver, and headed to the bayou for a little peace and calm water. The first morning was truly beautiful, the blur of isles were in the distance; birds danced about, and there was no need for shirt or shoes, no news of bombings, drives to the office or emails about contract negotiations.

There was just the heart and soul of the deep South for both us and the kids to absorb.

After preparing the boat, our family and the Morans were off on another adventure, this time heading out to the barrier islands off the Mississippi coast to see historic Fort Massachusetts on West Ship Island.

Not all of us were making the journey, however. For reasons that still baffle us, the older children had a way of disappearing whenever we mentioned seeing a historical site or national monument. They thought they were too cool while around their friends to be with parents and babies. They were up to nothing much or just planning on playing video games. As the older kids told us, "Nothing can go wrong, when will you be back?"

Tim Moran, our captain, liked to drive fast in his newly purchased Chris-Craft, and that day was no exception. With the kids packed in the front and back, baby Ellie clung to her mother as we sped along. Despite his penchant for great haste, Tim kept a close and careful eye on everyone.

The entire day was hot and humid, and the breeze on the boat was steady, keeping the heat at bay. A group of dolphins crested the skin of the water, charming us with their perfect arcs and elegance. I was sorry all the kids hadn't been there to see that.

About twelve miles off the coast, on the distant horizon, we all got the impression of land—a series of remote islands running along the southern seaboard, once providing safe harbors for pirates as well as sites for national defense, but which were now nationally protected seashores.

Speeding toward one of the islands, its colors seemed to burst forth—red brick, green grasses, white quartz sand and a brown dock, all under blue skies and bright yellow-white sunlight. While we tied up at the dock using a spider web of ropes and knots, a ranger provided suggestions and advice on how to tie the boat up properly.

As the kids offloaded at the southern end of the island,

the sun's heat absorbed in the tarred wooden planks kept them dancing until they got their shoes on. The long boardwalk extended from the dock to sugary beaches. And then the kids took off, leaving us parents slowly trailing behind. We stopped from time to time to look at what was right in front of us.

I was now facing the coast at the water's edge, and there stood Fort Massachusetts, an imposing structure. Construction of the massive brick fortification began in 1859. Its main level was adorned with gun ports placed alongside its curved stockade. Arched red-brick corridors connected the individual gun turrets, each protected by steel-shuttered cannon portals. Peering out through those narrow openings, I could easily imagine the range and trajectory of each cannon blast.

Climbing a courtyard stair tower to the fort's roof, we discovered it was covered with a protective layer of earth and grass. We were told that at key locations within the earthen barrier, massive cannons had once been placed to provide the fort added firepower. Near each defensive position were small doorways, which led to wood-lined powder magazines, where barrels of gunpowder and cannon-shot were once stored.

The thick brick structure was honeycombed with narrow stairwells leading down to the front's lower level. Still, those narrow passageways greeted us with cool air, just as 150 years ago they had greeted soldiers seeking an escape from the oppressive summer heat. The stairwell's stone steps were worn smooth, their once-sharp corners eroded from decades of footsteps.

The fort was the one constant on an ever-changing island often drenched and battered by both hurricanes and the onslaught of time.

We walked out of the fort's massive doors to the boardwalk's trail that lays a few feet above the coastal marshes, and we were bombarded by an assault of color and foliage—bright, beautiful greens from cordlike plants swaying to offshore winds. Tall sea oats sprang forth among the sand dunes, all of which were guarded by blue herons that stood tall. Offshore, the blue-green water lapped against a shoreline rich with crabs.

The afternoon sun had baked us, which we realized only as we boarded the boat and pulled away. As an added bonus, Hanna and Emma each got a Gulf Shore stamp, the first non-Olivia stamp in our family national park passport book. "Yes, life is good," I thought, staring back at the shoreline drifting out of view leaving it to solitude.

33 Johannesburg, South Africa

August 19, 2008

As I gazed at a sheet of paper, my pen ceased to function since my mind buzzed from the vibrating flight. I was overtired and not able to sleep. There were neither words nor counted sheep in the room as I sat alone and stared at the digital second-hand of the clock that blinked neon-green.

I had come to dread those excruciatingly long business trips which separated me from my family. Alone in a sterile room tucked away in a foreign land, all I loved so dearly was represented only by far-away voices on the other end of a telephone line.

Those trips broke our family rhythm, separating us for more than two weeks at a time. I missed Adam and Hanna's weekly tennis matches, the daily conversations with Anna—those exchanges so necessary for my soul—were now reduced to an occasional call, a text message or an e-mail.

I missed Olivia's supervision and her organization.

I missed Sofia's childlike love, which she extended when seeking our attention.

I missed my wife and Oliver next to me in the bed.

And now I sat there alone, the bedside clock ticking forward to one-thirty in the morning, and I wondered if my family missed me as much as I missed them. It was seven-thirty in the evening in Atlanta, not even on the same day. What a mess, this snapshot in my head. I could feel the insomnia, and

I knew I should take a sleeping pill or dial the phone to hear a familiar voice answer, then remind them I was gone.

I took the pill. Outside my window the moon was high. Johannesburg was boiling. Consumed by an eerie sensation, I felt as though the city was about to "run-amok" against itself at any moment.

In the morning, I woke, shaved at the sink, tied the knot on a silk tie, and two steps slower than usual, I went to the breakfast meeting in the lobby where well-dressed men wandered around, dragging themselves to taxicabs that would drive them through the ghetto streets and open market.

34 Three Days Later: Cape Town

August 22, 2008

Saturday at 9:30, I'd awakened in the Vineyard Hotel in Cape Town—my first real night's sleep in days.

The hotel was situated below Table Mountain, a noble massif of shale, granite and sandstone, some 900-million-years-old. The grounds were English garden landscapes that banked the crystal clear Liesbeek River where the lush leafy overgrowth ran along the water's perimeter. I walked the stone paths under the cover, a crown of golden fragrant flowers had burst into bloom, as if to seize life. Serenity was in abundance, provided by the gentle splashing of fountains next to the cascading river.

The ocean mist and Africa's rain touched every leaf and each blade of grass that morning, thoroughly shrouding Table Mountain, hiding its presence from the valley below. Only when the wind battered away the bleak covering of gray clouds did the mountain's naked peak appear only to then disappear.

Despite being surrounded by such elegance and charm, feeling not quite alive, I had a desire to embrace the tatter, to walk along the streets through the stale beer that recalled the party night before. A hotel car dropped me off at the Cape's waterfront, a commercial sort of place along a bay, where fishing boats were tied next to tourists' boats. Laborers were hard at work, repairing their tackle, as tour guides made last-minute calls for day-trippers.

Soon I was on Long and Kloof Streets—the exclusive section of town—where the tourist shops, bars and restaurants were in slumber, still trying to recover from last night's raucous parties. I could hear conversations from the windowsills, and the cigarette ashes dragged off red lips from the night before littered the gutters. There was a parked police car and a man with a pushcart full of mangos and newspapers moped along. I passed the national museums and universities; I ambled with no particular destination in mind, weaving in the multi-colored wave of the Cape's diversity.

And that was when I felt her eyes on me, a ghostly gaze from an alley-way.

She approached me—thin and soiled; her clothing nothing more than rags, she didn't smell like the flowers from the hotel garden; she smelled of the street. She wore the face of sickness and hunger.

"Please, do not judge me," she said in a raspy voice. "I am hungry. Can you buy me food?"

I blanked. She seemed so helpless, distressed, tired. I reached into my pocket and pulled out some rand. As I handed her the money, I felt a little better and a little sense of relief to see some of the anguish drain from her.

"Thank you."

"You're welcome. What's your name?" I responded, as if conversing with a new neighbor back home in Atlanta. I felt awkward and out of place, guilty.

Standing side-by-side amid the hustle, there was solitude within the Cape's tourist machinery; she told me her name. She was one of so very many, yet I had no idea what else I could do for her. I was afraid of her, not as though she would rob me, but afraid of that kind of grief and need and desolation. I gave her money, and I'd like to think that action helped her and maybe her family in some small way.

As I looked into her eyes, she again said, "Thank you, sir."

I turned away—for no good reason, other than feeling uncomfortable with the situation. And as I did so, I was immersed with shame, filth, the ugliness of judgment; I turned away with nothing but a hopeless hallucination of a home or a heaven where Jesus emerges from the tomb to relieve tears from Los Angeles to Golgotha. I took a cab back to the hotel.

I replaced the echoes of my solitude by going for a walk, substituting the dreary isolation of a hotel room with observations of the outside world.

Yet, on this next sojourn, I found myself walking through the streets where the privileged resided—each dwelling encircled by protective walls or electrified fences, which ensured seclusion and exclusion from outsiders; barriers marked by warning signs and topped by razor-wire and security lights—fortifications in supposedly civilized lands; castle-like structures where the only entrances were through massive gates or giant padlocked doors. I found a restaurant on a corner street and ate.

The next day, I went for a ride with a local, George, a friend and business associate who lived in the Cape; it was good to be poking around with someone I talked to each week on the phone. I had known George for about a year then, a very bright engineer who had talked me into purchasing manufacturing equipment in the Cape, and we were now working together to find opportunities.

It was a Sunday, and we traveled just outside of Cape Town, along the narrow, two-lane coastal road that gently bent and wove around mountain ranges and beach communities. It was here that I was greeted by varying elevations of nature's diversity, bordered by miles of largely unoccupied beaches. Only fearless surfers were present in the deep blue agitation of these shark-infested waters.

Mountains gave shade from the setting sun. These eastern slopes were less populated by vegetation and human settlement. High desert plains, with wind-blown undergrowth densely clustered together, afforded baboons protection from summer heat and coastal storms.

At the southernmost tip of Africa, the road lazily wound toward the mountain's precipice. High above us was a lighthouse. Exiting our vehicle, George and I entered an old cable-tram and made our ascent to the ominous and swaying creaking of antiquity.

And once this part of a perilous journey was over, all that remained was a steep climb up stone stairs to a panorama that was almost beyond description.

Far below, the western face of the mountain dropped straight to the ocean, where large rock formations served as a buffer against the violent crash of surf. As the massive ridge descended toward its southernmost point, the calm of the Indian Ocean collided with the powerful Atlantic in a disordered, white-capped cascade of swirling currents and waves.

In the Cape, there was a point in the swirling contrasts; in its social problems, classes, economy, distribution of resources, rivals between black and white, history of exploitation. Communities of people woke up from their comas and had no idea what the good things were anymore. What did all that have to do with me, the American that said the Lord's Prayer, had ambition, and who could buy what I needed? What I needed was cheap labor so I could compete with other U.S. companies that also bought cheap labor, here and in China and India. There must be a way to settle this supermarket so that the women I met on the street had opportunities to feel some good things and so that their future was not misguided by dark ages, some place, some world where she would not be forgotten by her family.

35 No Doubts

October 23–26, 2008

It was eye-opening to see Adam connecting the dots. He watched Anna read scripture, joined a church on his own earlier that year, and through Adam, we started our family's new journey with the Lord. He had become a man over that summer, and found love with Stephanie; his conversations required debate, and now he had deep views on the realities that surrounded him. In nature, he saw God's hand, that sureness that offers wisdom, and he knew all the rest would follow if he held on to that. His need to have and give joy could not be matched by anyone in our house. It was an exciting time, feeling my son make the most out of his life, seeing new attitudes, recalling my own. I found photographs of odd places we'd been, the kind that packed and unpacked memories.

We'd traveled that summer to Sweden, come back with more luggage than we took. In one of our carry-ons were several pieces of art collected over the years by Anna's father, Valdemar. The package sat in the plane's overhead bin—ordinary luggage.

Once we arrived home, I placed the package in the dining room, where it sat for a month. Finally getting around to taking a closer look at the artwork, I sat it on the table for viewing. There were two drawings that stood out. One was of an old man placing his hand on a boy's head as they knelt beside a body of water. On careful inspection, I noticed a signature below the bare foot of the bearded mentor. The second drawing was of an ice-skater wearing old wooden skates. A small inked stamp was next to the skater's foot.

Once both pieces were framed and hung in the dining

room, our "art viewing room" now, I could not help but admire the drawings' clean lines and attention to detail.

Later at work, I received a message to call Piyush—a close friend and past work-mate, an honest and kind gentleman. I had known him almost ten years, and he was my passage to India. Piyush was a father of three, two girls out of college and a son just beginning his second year at Emory.

As I made the call, little did I realize its importance would remain with me for the rest of my life. He had told me about a year before there was cancer, but his leaf had just fallen from the tree.

In a voice of pain and fatigue, Piyush told me he was in a hospice. I stopped what I was doing and rushed to his bedside. He was surrounded by his wife and children. Everyone was obviously drained by the ordeal of his battle, but all I could think of was finding a way to show this magnificent man how much I loved him, reciprocating the love he had shown me over the years.

In the course of my visit, I told Piyush about my family's recent trip to Sweden, about Hanna's and Adam's tennis matches—oh, how he loved to discuss tennis—and about the artwork we had brought back with us. It was just small-talk, really—anything other than discussing the proliferation of his necrotic cells. In fact, he even managed to smile when I mentioned that my recent research of two of the art pieces had revealed them to be etchings of some importance. I left his side in the early evening, promising to visit again.

The next morning I took the two etchings down and put them in the car. I had no idea why I did this, other than it seemed important that I show them to Piyush.

By the time I arrived at the hospice, the waiting room was overflowing with Piyush's friends and family—his brothers and sisters and in-laws. And on each of their faces was the devout love and concern for this special man.

Although Piyush was becoming weaker, it was obvious he was clinging to life for the sake of his family. In fact, months earlier he had told me, "I am okay with dying, except for leaving my family."

Seeing that I understood his struggle, he now asked, "Why is God doing this to me?"

My response was that which I'd told another dear dying friend a few years earlier: "He wants the good ones."

Of course, such a question made me wonder whether Piyush was grappling with his faith. And that was when I showed him the baptismal etching I'd brought to the hospice. When I set the artwork next to him, he took obvious pleasure in its promise—staring at it for long stretches, as though attempting to fully grasp its spiritual essence, as though he could feel that kind old man's hand against his own forehead. I'd thought of the artwork as nothing more than a diversion for my sick friend, as some way to have a normal conversation that didn't focus solely on his death.

The next day was Saturday—a solemn day. Although the sun was shining, its warmth was dissipated by high winds. When I returned to the hospice that morning, Piyush's family had not left his bedside. His spirit was growing weaker with each passing hour. And although he was moving closer to dying, I sensed he was still struggling as best he could to hang on to life. As though he was holding out for some specific day, though I am not sure he even knew what day it was.

It was an unusually cold and excruciatingly long day. I left late that night, after Piyush had said his final goodbyes.

The following day Piyush lay with eyes closed—his head propped high on pillows, his face sunken and drained. His wife Daksha brushed his hair as he slept through that Sunday. The rest of his family was nearby, refusing to end this vigil. Fear came over his children as the room seemed to get quieter and more peaceful, more still as Piyush's breaths grew quieter and less frequent.

And surely Piyush sensed all this, surrounded by all who trusted and loved him, as he started leaving this world and entering the next.

Daksha and their three children, Piyush's sister and I sat at a distance from Piyush until the nurse finally called us to his side. Only then did Piyush take his last breaths, and he was gone.

I'll never forget the screams from his children, trying to call their beloved daddy back to life.

Daksha was at her husband's side, a trembling hand caressing his body. Once the nurse arranged his body in repose, a silence hung over the room.

All we could do was hug, sharing each other's tears. I helped the family with the final arrangements, holding my own vigil as the funeral home's caretaker arrived and carried away my dear friend on a rolling stainless-steel gurney, his body covered by a white sheet.

Because he was to be cremated, Piyush's body was in a plain cardboard box the next day. At the funeral, there were pictures to remind us all of the joys and accomplishments of Piyush's life. Many friends spoke kindly of his generous and compassionate soul.

Following my own soul, I brought the baptismal etching that Piyush became so passionate about on his deathbed. Placing it gently next to him, I stepped away and shared with others my memories of Piyush. In return, they shared theirs with me as, individually, we struggled with our loss.

And then Piyush was reduced to ashes.

The artist was inspired to draw the etching while reading the following:

Acts 8:26–40

> And the angel of the Lord spoke to Philip, saying, Get up, and go toward the south unto the way that goes down from Jerusalem to Gaza, which is desert. And he got up and went: and, behold, a man of Ethiopia, a eunuch of great authority under Candace queen of the Ethiopians, who had the charge of all her treasure, and had come to Jerusa-

lem to worship, was returning, and sitting in
his chariot read Isaiah the prophet. Then the
Spirit said to Philip, Go near, and stay close
to this chariot. And Philip ran up to him, and
heard him reading the prophet Isaiah, and
said, Do you understand what you are reading? And he said, How can I, except someone
should guide me? And he invited Philip to
come up and sit with him. The place of the
scripture which he read was this,

"He was led as a sheep to the slaughter;
and like a lamb dumb before his shearer, so
opened he not his mouth: In his humiliation
his judgment was taken away: and who shall
declare his generation? For his life is taken
from the earth."

And the eunuch answered Philip, and said, I
ask you, of whom is the prophet speaking? Of
himself, or of some other man? Then Philip
opened his mouth, and began at the same
scripture, and preached to him Jesus. And as
they went on their way, they came to some
water: and the eunuch said, See, here is water; what keeps me from being baptized? And
Philip said, If you believe with all your heart,
you may. And he answered and said, I believe
that Jesus Christ is the Son of God. And he
commanded the chariot to stop: and they
both went down into the water, both Philip
and the eunuch; and Philip baptized him.
And when they came up out of the water, the
Spirit of the Lord caught away Philip, and
the eunuch saw him no more: but he went
on his way rejoicing. But Philip was found at

Azotus: and passing through he preached in
all the cities, till he came to Caesarea.

It all seemed so significant as I reflected on our children's
baptisms, all of them conducted at Anna's summer home on
the shores of Lake Hjälmaren. Each baptism tied us to the
heavens—so special, so gentle, so meaningful, a lifelong promise and memory of salvation for Adam, Hanna, Olivia, Sofia,
Anna and me.

Anna's father's art collection continued to bless us. Only
later did we discover the etchings were those of an Old Dutch
Master, this one above titled "Baptism of the Ethiopian Chamberlain." And how strange all these lives were woven together
by thin threads that took us on journeys, both physical and
spiritual, that shoved us towards purpose we didn't see coming
and didn't understand at the time.

Baptism of the Ethiopian Chamberlain,
Dutch. 1650-1655. Etching.

36 The Fall Tennis Season

September–November, 2008

It had been more than ten years since our Providence Lake tennis team last had a winning season. I was forty then, and we had to import Anna's nephew, Martin, from Sweden that year to sew up our success. Of course, Adam was on the sidelines, cheering us on to victory. He was eight and had just started playing tennis.

That spring of 2008 had been our worst season ever. All of us seemed too complacent, too lazy—maybe, God forbid, even too old. Even the most young-minded of us fretted that we were washed up. Our once-mighty serves had lost some zip, our footwork was footloose, and…well, there certainly was no arguing that none of us resembled those slick gentlemen staring back at us from that victorious 1997 team picture.

Vowing the 2009 season would be different, we altered the cast of characters—adding Michael Depeters, son of one of the teammates, he was two years older than Adam, and Michael brought along a college buddy, Wes. With some additional new-found neighbors, it proved to be a pretty good roster. The season started with a five-point victory. We won four matches the following week and three the week after. We were off and running.

What made this season even more special was that Adam turned eighteen just in time to join our team, in week two, which was an answer to a prayer right there. Ever since he first picked up a racket, I couldn't wait to team up with him on the court. And now it was happening—in a big way. Adam and Michael were our Young Guns—manning our No. 1 slot. Adam had a huge forehand and serve, and Michael's backhand was a motion of grace. This duo of action seldom dropped serve, kept the opponents moving, causing our opponents several forced errors and severe discomfort. It only took them the first match, which they lost in a three sets, to hone their partnership, but they rebounded the next week with a decisive victory and never looked back. I so wanted to insert myself as Adam's double partner, but never did, thinking it would be best for his self-assurance since he'd start college the next year. There would be plenty of seasons to play together, so I just enjoyed him being with me. Somehow all the pressure I put on Adam to play tennis seemed to vanish that season, he fulfilled my dreams, and I let it go on some abstract level.

Week after week they won with the confidence that only youth brings. And, better yet, Adam and Michael's prowess and spirit was so contagious that it lifted the rest of our team's play a notch or two. Overnight, Providence Lake had a team to be reckoned with.

I also held my own, playing mostly the No. 2 slot on the court next to Adam. All of which could be distracting at times, considering I'm one proud father. Playing my own shots with one eye while keeping the other focused on Adam's blistering serves or returns was no easy task. But I tried not to overdo it, attempting to keep my shouts of "Great shot, son!" or "Come on, Adam!" to a minimum.

The real beauty of this father–son "Mutual Admiration Society" was that each of our separate family victories created an ever-increasing bond. Michael and Adam always finished before me, and at the end of play, they came to the net, handshakes followed by, "Great match you played there," then Adam would turn to me and yell out, "Come on, Dad, I got the first point," or something else like that, and I just knew this was a place I could always come to with him.

I knew I was exceedingly tough on some of my teammates during our futile seasons, especially on my good friend Mason Holland. Even his wife, Stephanie, took some pleasure volleying verbal blows on her husband, following my suggested corrections to his game plan. But that's just my competitive nature, agonizing over every bad shot, every pathetic loss.

And now…well, the decade-long wait for such a spectacular season had been almost unbearable. It had been the object of my dreams—Adam and me, father and son, at center court, surrounded by the rest of these old tennis souls.

Of course, as much as we enjoyed our success, we certainly didn't allow it to go to our heads. We were far from pros. But we played for the pride of Providence Lake, which meant almost as much to us as Wimbledon did to Andy Roddick.

And pride of winning obviously also meant a lot to the team we'd soon be facing. In fact, the weekend before our final match, we discovered two unknown characters filming Adam and Michael. The spies turned out to be Jamaican table tennis champions, who we would soon take the court against.

We didn't know whether or not we were really *that* good. Good enough to inspire enough fear in the competition that they felt they had to scout and film us? Could that be possible?

Everything came down to the final weekend, the No. 1 and No. 2 teams playing at Providence Lake. If we won, we'd be division champions. Lose, and the other team advanced to the annual Atlanta Lawn Tennis Association playoffs.

Although Lou Depeters and I lost our match, Adam and Michael dazzled the opposition with their best performance of the season, thus securing for us the title. Game, set, and match—this, despite our opponents' trotting out a teaching professional across the net from Adam and Michael. Not that it mattered. Adam and Michael easily outpointed poor ethics and inferior sportsmanship. And besides one of these guys was a "table tennis" champion—a ping-pong star. But at the time, we didn't know enough to recognize or even consider that they wouldn't be as good with a "real" racket in their hand.

Our reward? As a team, we earned those cheap plastic bag tags, plus individual pride, which you can't buy at a trophy store. Adam hung his bag tag on an old wooden racket in his bedroom, equally as proud of his team as he was of himself. It still hangs on that racket.

It was the season of all tennis seasons. Although we advanced to the quarterfinals before losing, I got to witness first-hand the athletic maturation of my beloved son.

I couldn't help but believe a good man was in the making.

37 Purpose

Adam liked to tell stories all the time, and they had a meaning to him and to those who got to hear and be characters in them. The following passages were some of the stories he told, they came from a personal journal he wrote for a school assignment:

"Let's see, well, I was a rather cute little boy when I was in elementary school. I was kind-hearted boy, I did everything that I was told, obeyed orders and did all of my work. In my middle school years, I became more a nerd. I had an obsession with video games, when I got home that would be the first thing that I'd do. I know it sounds dumb don't make fun of me.

My favorite class in elementary school was recess. If I do recall correctly and I do, my most enjoyed time in school was snack time along with recesses. I enjoyed snack time so much because I got hungry in school and I would snack just in time to fill me up. I loved recesses because it was an opportunity to communicate and enjoy activities with my companions. My favorite activity was kickball, back in the day I played that game just about every day. I was amazing. I was known for my radical pitches they were crazy. And another missed pastime, was naptime. I wish we still had nap time because it would give me an excuse to sleep in school.

My first crush well I guess it would be with a girl who I met in elementary school. Her name was Shannon Thompson, she was more like a best friend than a crush. We sat at the lunch table together and we sat in every class together. Then one day she moved and I never saw or heard of her again. Until one day I was on Facebook and I had a new friend request, it was her. I accepted it as soon as I saw who it was, I talked to her and she turned out to be a writer, she wrote books that were being sold on the net.

The most beneficial thing that I have in school would be my study skills class. In this class I have time to complete all of my homework. I do all my homework in this class so that I don't have to do it at home. I learned about good study habits and bad ones. I learned how the brain works it's an awesome class.

In high school I couldn't wait to get a car it would be so cool to drive and pull up to school in my car. I was eager to meet new people and experience new things. I was scared of all the work that I would get in school but it wasn't that bad. I thought of all the girls that I would see. O yea I was scared that there would be a big bully. I thought there would be secret meetings in the bathroom. I wondered what group of people I would be associated with. I thought of the football games that I would go to. I dreamed of playing on the high school tennis team.

My best memories in high school are the people. Then one day I met this most beautiful girl her name was Stephanie. Little did I know that I would become madly in love with this girl. She became my girlfriend and I felt love for the first time in my life.

I continue to grow. What will happen with my life? Well, when I get out of high school I will go to Georgia Tech and major in electrical engineering. Then I will get a job with Intel designing and manufacturing processors. I will make loads of money, this is my dream job and I would love to have it as a profession.

Looking back I wouldn't change much, well come to think about it I wouldn't change anything because if I changed all that stuff I probably wouldn't be having the best years of my life. Come on, look at me, I am in love and that would have never have happened to me if I changed my past."

There were the times he'd just tell his mother, "Good night, love you," walking out of the bathroom, towel wrapped around his waist, dripping from the shower. She'd sit up in the bed and say, "Love you, Dukee," using the pet name she gave him when he was just a baby.

I was watching Adam grow all those years. I was blown away by how fast this had all happened.

In the meantime, I was aging gracefully, and my work continued to be rewarding. More than anything else, though, my priority continued to be my family—the most important aspect of my life. I've been blessed—a beautiful and loving wife, and four adoring children. No father could have asked for more.

But, admittedly, there was an area in which I'd been quite negligent. Although my Anna had always been spiritual-minded, and then Adam followed her in that, I'd never really made that commitment on my own part. I'd found myself wondering about the origin of life, but it was something I took for granted—leaning on my collegiate teaching that it was simply a matter of chemical evolution: Stars shine brightly and their mere mass kept surrounding planets in order, and when time and space were just right, life took hold. On ocean floors, warm water flowed from protrusions, where geysers of heat provided needed nutrients, supporting a bacterium, which, in turn, became a tubeworm or a clam, thus allowing life to take hold. I viewed nature as a pure form of life—the tree stood tall year after year, bearing fruit and seeds, which eventually fell to the ground and lay dormant until the combination of soil, rain and light caused new growth. That was the way it was. The way life began and moved forward—the birds and the bees and all that.

But then, enduring the joys and sorrows of fatherhood,

questions took root. Was Adam and Eve nothing but a Bible story, just reading to some, or could it be that God turned them loose in a garden to name animals and enjoy it, except for that damn tree?

A man and woman went for a roll and soon baby makes three (or four for them). Time passed, the purpose of nature's simplest interactions became too complex as we re-established and re-assembled our unnatural worlds.

And, as we sat in wonder, our minds groping for answers, answers which were not always apparent, our hearts led us to a belief in a higher power. Perhaps it came from a need to know that there was something greater out there than just "us" or what we could reach out and grab with our hands. I read the Bible from beginning to end, and found myself rejoicing and comforted by its teachings and my time in prayer. Souls were at rest, satisfied with a conclusion, while life moved ever forward, coming and going from place to place—its creator never still for too long.

Nature, by its very being, had a way of informing us of its simple demands, like the sun reflecting off rain clouds, meadows without flowers, a rainbow faith vision.

Yet, faith is not always understood.

While I pondered the differences and demands which give mankind principle, it became obvious that each of us must examine what it is that is dearest to our hearts, then pursue it with honest purpose, in a manner void of serving the self.

Although I was content to be cherished first and foremost as a father, I knew those who lived a hollow existence, who went about their lives alone—worshipping a career, forever seeking praise and their twisted concept of success, constantly comparing their existence to that of others, as if it were a contest of greed, always looking down when they should be looking up.

But most of all, we need more families that lovingly embrace each other for better or worse, families that refuse to break the cherished bond, no matter what—from day to day, not just when it is merely convenient for holiday schedules.

I chose to believe that the origin of life was as pure and simple as a seed—a leaf on a tree; a forest with free-flowing creeks, where wildflowers grow as seasons change with the revolution of the planet around a shining star. Thus we live together within a nature, where higher powers provide aspirations. And while this absolute understanding may not be worldly, I am content to believe we strive with a devotion to our heart's purpose, "Here on Earth, as it is in heaven."

38 One Day of Life

December 1, 2008

It was Monday evening, and I was thankful for all that God had blessed me with. Our home had a simple love within it, a love that made us happy.

Anna and I had been married twenty-two years, and that night we were drinking our tea together in the living room where Adam had made a fire. Of course, Anna believed he hadn't used the piped-in gas to start such a billowing flame. But when she finally figured it out, she accused him of cheating.

I smiled. It was a relief to hear Anna enforce her Swedish fire-building techniques (which included paper, kindling and matches) on someone besides me. Something she felt the need to impart prior to the lighting of any fire, although she never seemed to put into practice those techniques herself.

Turning my attention to the rest of the family, there was no escaping the melodic strains emanating from Sofia's violin; the annual fifth grade concert was in three days, and I was eagerly awaiting her performance. And when Hanna entered the room to warm herself by the fire, I read her one of my short chapters. Although she seemed to enjoy it, you just never knew what was going on in the mind of a teenager.

Nonetheless, this was a pleasant respite from news that I'd gotten earlier in the day. I'd received word that Rob Hector, one of the company's stockholders had killed himself. This was the second father in such a short time to leave his family, Piyush's death having occurred so recently; I thought of Rob's wife Nancy and their three children. I felt for her and her young kids, who would unfairly carry the type of pointless guilt that suicide often brings.

For some, life can become too much to bear. I was struck by the realization that reality was not absolute, but a place where someone could jump off a bridge, cut his wrist, overdose, all because the person knew life was hysterical, that it battered his brain, and because his family or loved ones weren't enough, or maybe they felt like too much.

I believed in faith and goodwill—prayed it was just around the next corner.

While our children were not oblivious to the distress going on around them, Anna and I kept things upbeat, reminding them of the value of being a close-knit family—making the most of what oftentimes had been a depressing holiday season, muddling through it with grateful hearts, ever thankful for all we'd been blessed with.

As always, Anna was a constant. She had gone into a cooking/baking mode. She baked breads that filled the rooms with the smell of warm grains. We tasted cookies—all simple, comforting foods. We had felt a little entitled over the years, but now a little humility was being served. I knew we would all grow from this.

39 New Year's, 2009

January 1, 2009

Sitting at the Morans' breakfast counter with this sweet redhead, I was nursing a cup of coffee she gave me to keep me warm, while surveying the carnage from the night before.

We were in Washington D.C., staying with our good friends Megan and Tim Moran, and the first day of 2009 greeted me with high winds and bitter cold. Not to mention confetti. Flashes of blue, orange, red, yellow and pink were everywhere. Scattered among this paper shrapnel were top hats adorned with the usual New Year greetings, empty poppers, and ribbon streamers stretching from floor to ceiling. A pointy party-hat sat on the counter, its silver tassels limp and hung-over from a late night of merrymaking, and every inch of the table top was covered with half-full plates of food and half-empty glasses and bottles.

My mind was still asleep. I took another sip of coffee. And then another. I found myself wondering about the past year, our travels, how we connected as a family, met up with some dreams, answered some questions about each other, established ourselves through God's nature. Then when I thought about the death of fathers, I was drenched by the weight where souls were taken and remembered children grieving, calling for their father, though they did not know what lay for them behind the next door. There was so much baggage from the past year, and I was nervous about carrying luggage from place to place.

My solace was broken by the sound of feet shuffling across floorboards and carpet.

It was about time; the rest of the house was slowly break-

ing free of their slumber, coming to join me for coffee and...
no, it was the children, and they seem baffled that no one was
keeping a close eye on them.

Little Ellie picked up a handful of rainbow-colored streamers and started running in circles, encouraging her brothers
and sisters to join her celebration. She was making amends for
last night, when she almost managed to make it to midnight's
explosion of colors and sounds.

Tommy, this little red-headed trouble maker, walked in
with two huge bags of cookies. I could tell by his sly smile that
he knew he had but a brief opportunity to gorge himself without fear of reprimand, which he did, heartily, before dropping
his goodies and retreating to a distant room as, at long last, the
rest of the adults slowly made their way into the kitchen.

There was more coffee, friendly smiles and more New Year
greetings, yet obviously not as boisterous as those extended
hours earlier.

And then, once everyone was satisfied that they indeed
had a pulse, the clean-up began. Piles of color were swept
away, tables and chairs were re-arranged. Brooms, vacuums
and trash bags replaced the tables of food and spirits, and the
joyous merrymakers who, hours earlier, had gathered around
them.

The night before the guests, with children in tow, had
started to fill the house around seven P.M. Without pause, the
kids scurried off to their party domain on the first and third
floors.

This gathering was long on tradition. On the last day of
December these special friends met and greeted every New
Year under a sea of balloons Tim had carefully arranged. And
while he was also taking delight in the precise placement and
lighting of the candles, Megan ensured that every other detail
was attended to, always with at least two or three of the children close by her side.

Anna and I were content to mingle, still somewhat amazed
that earlier in the day, while jostling our way through what

seemed like thousands of shoppers at a nearby mall, we ran into Carmo and Dave Boss, our old next-door neighbors. Indeed, what a small world it is. We enjoyed a drink together and reminisced, then said our goodbyes in order to say hello to the New Year.

And so the party began.

Waiters served appetizers and filled glasses with ice, then mixed in rums and whiskeys. The room was bathed in the raucous strains of music, yet it seemed as if only Adam and Anna were in the mood for dancing, when Freddy Mercury and David Bowie's "Under Pressure," began to play. I couldn't begin to tell you how happy I was to see my son dancing with his mother. I sat on the couch and watched. When they finished, Adam plopped down next to me. He was so close I could feel the heat of his body, and someone snapped a picture. Anna was off looking for a drink. He said, "All is ready for the fireworks, could be some rain," then he told me some joke. We laughed, and shared a drink later outside on the deck, where girls were drunk and happy.

As the hours wore on, guests came and went as the year ticked toward its demise. And then, as the end-hour approached, someone turned up the volume as Tim's arrangement of songs played on. Everyone gathered in the family room around the ones they knew or wanted to know, and the countdown began…Ten…nine …eight… After, everyone drank champagne, gave hugs and kisses—fully embracing 2009!

Adam and I had our own tradition outside in the cold— setting off fireworks. Soon the sounds and sights of our pyrotechnics interrupted the merrymaking, and the party moved to the front porch to watch the confetti-filled sky.

Once we'd fired off the last bottle rocket, the party began to wind down. Tim's office was stacked high with jackets, scarves and hats, all of which were retrieved as other guests searched for family members lost to the floors above and below. Finally, amid the celebration's debris, Tim and Megan stood at the front door and bid one and all a heartfelt: "Good night and Happy New Year."

As the last party-goers departed, Megan's relief was obvious.

40 *Get Low*

March 1–5, 2009

It was not exactly the type of weather Hollywood had in mind when it decided to film the movie *Get Low* in the sunny South, but no one seemed to mind.

Despite that Saturday's bitter cold and a forecast of four- to six-inches of snow over the next four or five days in Atlanta—in March, no less—Tim Moran and his son, Tommy, plus me and my entire family met at Ted's Grill to have lunch with Dean Zanuck, the movie's producer.

Many times, I was almost tempted to ask Anna to pinch me, just to make sure I wasn't dreaming. Not only were we lunching with one of Hollywood's elite, but in the upcoming days, Tim, having pulled a few strings, had arranged for all of us to be extras in a pivotal scene in the movie.

Although at that point we had not yet met the stars of the film—Robert Duvall, Sissy Spacek, Bill Murray and Lucas Black—I was struck by how down-to-earth Dean Zanuck was. A gentle, soft-spoken man, he was completely at ease as he talked with everyone at the table, including our children. I couldn't help but marvel at his thoughtful consideration, humility and kindness, especially for one in such a stressful occupation.

After lunch we dropped Dean off at his hotel, and drove over to the movie site to take a quick look around. The filming was taking place about fourteen miles west of Marietta at the Pickett's Mill Battlefield Historical Site, where the Confederate Army defeated Union forces on May 27, 1864. The evening's cold, hard winds and ominous clouds cut short our excursion, so we turned around and headed home. We'd already been told that we'd need a good night's sleep to prepare us for tomorrow's activities. It proved to be a wise decision.

Sunday was a bit more tolerable, considering the weather. We spent most of the day standing in various lines or in tents, being fitted and refitted in 1930s-era outfits by wardrobe artists Julie and Dan. I can't speak for everyone else, but to me, this life-as-a-movie-extra seemed to take forever.

The girls went first—a dress here, a hat there, then shoes and coats—all coordinated and harmonized to Julie or Dan's vision. Once the descriptive paperwork was tabulated for each picture-perfect ensemble, someone assigned a number to it and its respective character. When it was my turn to be fitted, Julie took a quick look and then told me to wear my best black suit and a white shirt with no buttons on the collar. She also gave me a well-used, yet colorful tie, a hat and the heaviest coat I've ever held.

Since Adam missed the fitting because of his church obligations, Tim and I returned with him Monday. It proved to be quite an experience because Adam was selected to play the role of a young bombardier, complete with a leather coat lined with a sheepskin collar and cuffs, and ill-fitting brown trousers, intentionally chosen to show a gap between the cuffs and his black shoes. Dan had Adam augment the outfit with a derby cap.

So stunning was the ensemble, that Julie later said, "You look remarkable. Who arranged your outfit?"

Dan heard her compliment.

Tim, Adam and I drove over to meet up with Dean, who was overseeing a film sequence using a refurbished log cabin tucked back in the woods. The one-room dwelling, complete with a stacked-stone chimney, had two small wooden porches that were lit so brightly that its intensity felt unnatural for shaded forest.

"We had to build that small barn and a mule corral," Dean told us. Both buildings were littered with rustic tools, thus completing the reclusive-looking setting. Of course, at odds with the deep woods was the vast array of technology—cameras, sound equipment, lights, production and mixing boards—all of which were arranged in precise pecking order, ensuring a timely production.

I was about to tell Tim that these Hollywood folks had everything figured out, when first the rain and then the snow began blanketing everything. Problematic, yes—but not when you're dealing with A-list actors. It was almost as if both Robert Duvall and Bill Murray had shouted, "The show must go on." They continued performing, without complaint, through the dreary mess. It was extraordinary, indeed, to see these stars finish their scenes without a hitch, both inside and outside the cabin.

And while I gushed at the professionalism of these two headliners, Adam acted as if he had no idea who they were, proving to me, once again, that he had a special desire to work in the field of engineering. He reserved all his enthusiasm for the production's technology. No surprise, considering he'd be studying computer science when he entered college the following year.

Tuesday we woke to a Southern rarity—a thick snow, which was great for kids of all ages, including Hollywood moguls. And everything sparkled merrily and was good.

So, as expected, it was a work day—an early work day, for that matter—we had to be on the movie set by five A.M. Rising early was one thing, enduring what would prove to be one of the coldest days in recent memory was yet another.

We drove in darkness, parking on the abandoned drag strip alongside hundreds of other vehicles. In front of us were illuminated tents where about one-hundred other extras were all shivering as they stood in line waiting for their bureaucratic paperwork, wardrobe, or make-up and hair styling.

Tim Moran and I were the only ones who had their kids with them, all of whom were wide-eyed with equal parts curiosity and awe. Of course, their excitement was contagious.

Tim and I were also on edge—such was the hypnotic power of being on a movie set.

Like everyone else, I was freezing. So, in hopes of finding a little warmth, I eased on over to the make-up tent, where I knew I'd find my girls. After all, when it came to putting on make-up, everyone knew it was a prolonged process with the softer set. And sure enough, that was where I found Hanna, Sofia, Olivia and Tim's daughter, Emma, who had arrived from Washington D.C. the day before.

"Where's your mother?" I asked Adam, who responded with a knowing smile.

Nearby was a white-haired lady, adorned in a blue dress and looking at herself in a mirror. I could see her reflection, and could tell she was not at all pleased with my being there.

I turned away and asked Tim, "Have you seen Anna around?"

He looked stunned. Silence prevailed. And then, upon closer inspection, I discovered that the old lady was Anna. Oh, my God, she was fuming—either at me, or the production crew's decision to have her cast as an old, worn out wife, a most senior citizen.

I stepped outside the tent and into the freezing morning air, seeking solace, wondering if this was a premonition of our growing old together.

The rising sun provided no warmth. Everyone was standing in an open field, buffeted by a brisk breeze. Scattered around us were older model cars from the 1920s and '30s, among them a black hearse with a coffin inside. Against the backdrop of a raised wooden stage, fire pits were burning. The field was surrounded by tall Georgia pines, which did little to cut the wind.

Our girls, clad only in their dresses, hovered close to rusted metal barrels piped with gas burners. Although these provided a little heat, Olivia seemed the worse for wear—her face hauntingly white as she shivered in a little green dress with matching hat and strappy shoes.

Once filming got underway, Olivia and Adam seemed to be intentionally selected by the crew for a sentimental scene, where, in dawn's light, they were walking in the early morning to Felix Bush's (played by Robert Duvall) planned funeral. Bush was a Tennessee recluse, who needed to set the wrongs of his past right. It was a fable of real life where his loneness was self-induced, a true story for many who reflect on their days here on earth, who know death comes to us all. So get it right when you have the chance, and Bush was doing just that.

Watching my children walking down the dirt road into the woods, I was reminded of my father, wishing we had set certain things right without judgment hanging over us. I needed mercy and forgiveness, so I could put what was bad about us behind me and maybe behind us both. Although there was a surreal quality about the scene, it proved difficult to attain Zanuck's perfection. Three takes, then a fourth before everyone was pleased. And once the filming was completed, Bill Murray approached my freezing little girl and offered her his coat. Olivia's smile of gratitude was so captivating that Murray called for someone to bring her some warm boots.

And as she warmed to his thoughtfulness and consideration, he talked to Olivia about the nothings you talk about when you meet children for the first time. He still wasn't done, though. Throughout the rest of the day he gave Olivia special attention—a chat here, a joke there. It was an experience she'll never forget.

At the end of the day, Olivia was cast with Tim's son, Tommy, in an impromptu scene where he walked over to Olivia, as if to tell her some deep secret. As she bent down to Tommy, who was younger and much shorter, he buried a kiss on her cheek.

That alone was an experience of a lifetime for two very proud fathers and their families. And from the expressions of delight on Olivia and Tommy's faces, it was a moving experience for them also.

It was fantastic for the kids to see the dedication, detail, work and focus of a team of actors, crew, and so many others, as they connected in the filming of a project. Two of the scenes took more than twelve hours to complete—a freezing joy of sorts. The best part was the unselfishness and kindheartedness that our kids experienced while actually working on a movie set. Murray came over to Olivia at the end of the day and gave her his call sheet, a detailed page of information that actors get each day. It was autographed by all the stars appearing in that scene. Also, earlier in the day, maybe helping my cause a bit, Murray made Anna feel much younger by telling her, "You are good at making babies."

41 Forgiveness & Death

I took a flight to San Diego for Mother's Day 2009 and checked into a La Jolla hotel. I needed solitude and some time to think before I saw my mother. It had been many years since our last face-to-face. And I'd been thinking about our past—a series of gestures and pushing-aways—steps and missteps and then all that time and space separating us. But I wanted to see her again, perhaps just to see if things would really be the way they had always been. I think I was hoping for change, but realistically knew to not expect that exactly.

Lynn stopped by the hotel the afternoon I arrived. She said she just wanted to check out my accommodations, when, in truth, she wanted to see me. This was her roundabout way of connecting with me, and I welcomed that connection. When I told her about my plans to see our mother, I asked, "Would you like to have lunch with us or something?"

She reacted as anticipated—she was astounded by the mere fact that I would suggest such a thing. Her psychologist told her, "If unhappy, put up acceptable barriers," which Lynn believed were needed. I understood.

"I already have plans to be with Roger's family," she said, then went into an elaborate and lengthy explanation, including details about all of her husband's relatives who would be in attendance.

I'd known all along I'd be flying solo on this kamikaze mission. Little wonder, because our mother's abuse of family and friends always made visits infrequent and painful. We all knew what to expect.

The next morning I drove to my mother's rundown apartment complex, adjacent to a major freeway. Heat waves rose off the bleached concrete roadway, and the smell of car exhaust floated in the air.

When my mother answered the door, the stench of alcohol and cigarette smoke gushed forward, as if escaping a sick room. She had made an effort to pull herself together, but decades of abuse had taken their toll. Her eyes, a little crazy and red, were covered with smudged, oversized glasses. Her hands shook; her face was wrinkled from age, and her hair was spotty in places. Her once-sharp mind that had helped me with homework was now drenched from decades of alcohol abuse. It wasn't easy to overlook her diseased condition, but I was there to neither criticize nor judge, as difficult as that was. After all, it was Mother's Day. I was curious as to whether or not she remembered that.

"Are you ready to go?"

"Where are we going?"

"Wherever you'd like."

"Well, it's been so long since I've been to the Hotel Del Coronado. My bridge tournaments were there, and I ate in the expensive dining room downstairs, you know." I wanted the trip to be special to her, and it didn't surprise me that she tried to recreate something she remembered as her glory days.

I could see she had this desire to relive her past. As I drove along the freeway and over the Bay Bridge, she asked, "Why are we not taking the ferries?"

I didn't dare reply. The car ferries had stopped operating forty years ago—about the time my mother lost contact with reality.

I wasn't going to be the one to tell her about the ferries.

Once we arrived at the Coronado, she was ecstatic when the doorman opened the car door for her. She exited the vehicle and stepped onto the red carpet as if awaiting applause for her triumphant return. I assisted her up the stairs and into the dining room of her satiated yesterdays, where a white-dressed hostess kindly arranged a window seat overlooking the ocean and a well-manicured garden.

We started with coffee served in china cups, followed by the hotel's annual Mother's Day brunch. We sat and talked for a couple of hours about the kids, and Adam and Hanna's tennis. She reminded me her father had been the Illinois Senior State Champion. I told her Adam joined a church and that we'd all started going and that he'd be off to college the next fall. It was awkward. She repeated herself, forgot the kids' names. I told her James was having problems, and she asked what I was doing to help him, but before I could answer, she said, "He'll be just fine after he gets rid of his wife. Make sure you help him do that."

"She's the saint in this one, and the kids need both of them," I replied. There was no way and really no reason for me to try to convince her of anything. She was just holding on, asking about the crab, eggs Benedict, wondering if she should get a waffle, asking for some champagne.

I told her, "Have it all. I came here on Mother's Day just to see you."

She smiled, felt noble for a moment. There was a break in the conversation, and I took a drink of coffee, set it down, stirred the spoon against the cup, tapped it, set it on the saucer, then, looking into her eyes, told her, "I love you and forgive you."

Her reaction was reserved, almost dismissive—as if she could not comprehend what it was about her lifestyle that needed forgiveness. "I don't need your forgiveness, John."

"Ok, but I needed to say it." I knew she did not understand how important this was to me, to our troubled past or to God, so we left it that way.

Near the conclusion of our brunch, over dessert, I told her about my family's visit to Chicago. Told her about how cold it was, how we almost lost the family to a blizzard, saw the Nutcracker, and told her about our visit with her younger sister Susan. There was some small talk about Susan's house, and she asked, "Is she was still married to John?"

I said, "Yes, and we spoke about David." She took a gulp of the champagne and looked down at the table.

I took the opportunity, and taking a deep breath, said something I'd rehearsed, "I learned the truth about your brother's homosexuality and the circumstances surrounding his suicide. So, why did you lie about Uncle David's lifestyle and death to me?" I picked up the spoon, stirring again.

My mother simply stared at me. A minute passed before she barked out, "Susan is a bitch and a liar."

And so ended my cross-country quest of absolution. There were no more healing words; no hugs, no kisses, no understanding whatsoever. I paid the check, assisted Mother to the car amid the noxious fumes of her perpetual cigarette, then made the uncomfortable return drive toward her public-housing hole of unremitting degradation.

As I walked her to the door, she said, "Thank you again for the Mother's Day brunch. I'm so tired, son. I have to take a nap."

She left me with one last little lie before consuming her next drink; she wouldn't be taking that nap.

Monday and early morning Tuesday
—May 11–12, 2009

I checked out of the hotel the next morning and met up with Ken Garry, a high school buddy. We were attending an engineering meeting that Monday morning, and the plan called for me to spend the rest of the evening in his "Granny room," which was separated from his home by a small court-yard.

It's uncanny how enduring friendship can be. We met in high school, more than thirty years ago, and now we were working together on my new project. Ken and his wife Melody had a young son, Hayden, who was about ten.

Instead of dining with them that night, however, I drove over to Bill and Carol Burnell's home and spent the better part of the evening with them. Our friendship had been rekindled since my family and I had traveled to Pittsburgh to attend their son's wedding. Carol prepared an elegant dinner, which we ate outside, and afterwards I returned to the "Granny room" to get some sleep, which I felt I needed to put Mother's Day behind me.

I laid down, knowing I missed Anna's Mother's Day back home, and missed how Adam gave her Good and Plenty's, missed the cards, all handmade, set out on the table, and their dinner together was without me.

The TV was not working, and so with my mind on nothing in particular, soon I was asleep. For some reason, I was jarred awake at two-thirty in the morning, West Coast time. It felt as if an unseen hand had suddenly rousted me out of bed. Trying to ease myself back to sleep, I picked up a book I'd brought, given to me more than ten years ago by Dr. Long, who was like a father, the only man I knew that had true politeness. I feared him in high school, we all did, he was a ball-buster, but we had worked together for almost eighteen years since then. He'd recently passed away due to complications from an infectious disease and cancer, and I missed him. I tried reading myself back to sleep, but sleep was impossible. It wasn't that I had something on my mind, it felt more like, *Why am I here?*

And then I heard a phone ringing. It was still quite late or early—it depends on how you put it, but still there was silence for several minutes following the ringing.

Then there was a knock at my door. Pushing through the quiet and opening the door, I knew immediately that something was terribly wrong. Melody tried not to look me in the eye, and I could see the pain etched into her face. I felt myself go very still.

"You need to call home," she said.

With an unsteady hand, I reached for the phone and dialed our number. Anna answered. I was greeted by the most haunting cry I had ever heard, and then her screaming, "Adam is gone. He was killed in a car crash."

I had trouble breathing. Anna continued to sob into the phone.

"Are you sure?"

"He is gone," she said. "Come home."

At first, I had no words. But when I started to wail, "No, please, not Adam; please, Lord, no—not him." The line went dead.

God had abandoned me. Time stopped. I was cold. Numb and still in disbelief. Surely, they'd gotten this wrong. I was buried under an avalanche, all was dark.

I called home again. The screams and crying of our children—Hanna, Olivia and Sofia—forced me onto my knees, their cries felt like they were echoing inside me, reverberating, helpless, helpless, helpless: "I want Adam back. I want Adam back. Adam, come back."

Little Sofia did not know what to do. "I miss Adam," she told me through her tears. "I want him back, Daddy." I could not give her that. I was her father and would give her anything, but she asked for the one thing I could not give.

I was incapable of responding, other than to say, "I love you. I'll be home soon."

And then I curled into a ball in the corner of the room and cried for my son. Ken came to me—to offer me comfort. I tried to stand, then collapsed in his arms.

Someone called my sister, and Lynn made arrangements for me on the first flight home. I wished she had gotten on that plane with me. I had a row to myself, kept my face planted in a pillow against the inside of the plane, the flight crew knew what had happened and protected me. Four hours. I felt as if my life had become unbearable and meaningless, if not merciless. I wanted to die, so I could be with Adam in heaven, where I knew he surely was.

Death had walked through my door and into my house, and bludgeoned me and my family without mercy. In a moment of philosophical clarity, I realized that all relationships were temporary, that death was as common as life itself.

But in another moment, I was consumed with righteous anger, screaming inside: If anyone must die, it should have been me—not Adam!

All that remained was a gloom that went beyond mere sadness, a pain that felt more than simply mental but was physical. And my tears, my tears remained. My mind continued to race, the thoughts tortuous: "No, this is so bad. This is so bad. No, please. This is so bad. This is so bad. No, please. This is so bad."

My love for Adam knows no limit. I stared at his pictures and read and reread his last text message to me, which remains saved on my phone.

I did this over and over, repeating to myself, "This is so bad. No, please," then the plane landed after an eternity.

Tim Moran must have dropped everything and flown down from D.C. He was at the airport waiting for me, such a good man. We took a cab back to the house, a white cross was being cemented in on New Providence Road, TV crews and people everywhere. There were more at the house. I went in, held Anna. We cried, it did not stop. The girls, all wet faces, I kissed them. Their girlfriends were there, doing all they could to assure them. I went to Adam's room. It was packed with faces I knew. It was silent, I saw Stephanie, held her, and I hoped she was pregnant. I sat down at his desk, ran my fingers over his things.

Then I got one of his friends, took him outside, asked him, "Can you drive me to a place?"

"Where are we going?"

"I'll tell you when we get in the car; I'll be out front in a minute, down by the path."

This boy, Adam's age, drove me to the darkest room in the world, where Adam lay. I wondered if Adam was cold, and he was. All I could think was that he was so cold, and that I needed to get him warm. I kissed him, held his feet, kissed them too, cut a lock of hair; I did not want to leave him alone. But I had gone missing too, I went home, took out a suit and the best pair of shoes and told Anna we must go.

ADAM

Oh, Son. Oh, Son, our firstborn.
Our time was short.
Pure in mind and thought are you.
Your sweetness, happiness, goodness and love, a delight.
Your smile will never fade; your soul will never fail.
In heaven you wait, all in white.
Oh dark, oh dark is my heavy heart.

September 23, 1990–May 12, 2009

Adam showed me how to be a father, how to love unconditionally, he brought our family to the Lord, and he provided us with our greatest tragedy. Adam, I love you. I love you. Fathers should die before sons. I will never forget how you called me Papa.

42 No Mercy in Life

June 3, 2009

I could be a vindictive man. I could hate. I could carry that coffin the rest of my life. I could wrap my mind around the concept of revenge; my pain was that great those days. I went through the greater part of my life accepting faith, treating the ones around me with flawed and imperfect intentions, hoping for a higher purpose. Life always had these two edges for me.

But then my world was damaged, altered by the unfortunate turn of a steering wheel that was within the grasp of a teenage drunk driver. An automobile left the road, hit a telephone pole, and the victim was the vehicle's innocent passenger who just happened to be my son and the only one wearing a seat belt.

And it was surreal to have gotten the call from the District Attorney's office, requesting my presence in court. It had only been twenty-two days since Adam was killed. Our family was still in mourning. There was no sunshine, only despair, and I suspected I'd always be in mourning—how could I think otherwise?

Yet, the disturbing and despicable antics during the early stages of this trial became my new reality. Andrew London, the driver, pled "not guilty," then his attorney requested his release without bail. I got up, said a few words, and they gave him bail with house arrest.

I became quite familiar with the cast of characters. I saw them during the day at court, then again at night, during my seemingly endless nightmares. At court, there was the police lieutenant who arrived at our house on that fateful night and hesitantly informed Anna that Adam had been killed; there were the DAs, accompanied by their staff; there was the nineteen-year-old Andrew who was behind the wheel of the death car and had been behind bars an hour earlier, facing nine charges, including DUI homicide; and accompanying him was the self-proclaimed Pastor and his ditzy wife. They flanked their son, the so-called deacon of their disingenuous church. This pastor had used his children to gather parishioners like my son, with the hope the children would bring their friends and their tithing parents, who eventually must show up to see what is going on, under his leaking roof.

It was so difficult for me to keep my focus; it was hard for me to keep from crying. Everyone and everything seemed so distant, so out of touch, plastic people in an artificial setting, with no real concern for my grief.

As we waited to enter the courthouse, Andrew's mother merely stood off to the side, at arm's length. She was looking directly at me, sporting the same smile she displayed in church.

My God, why was she smiling at me? Didn't she realize my pain or that her son, if convicted of killing my son, would be facing years in prison?

Maybe she was incapable of recognizing others' pain. I certainly didn't resemble the man I was twenty-three days ago. I'd aged, dramatically. My eyes were red from the constant tears; my once-persistent grin had become a frown or a look of bewilderment. It was impossible to keep my chin up because I couldn't keep my head from drooping as I sought solitude.

I turned away from her, my head bowed in silence. Minutes ticked. I took a deep breath and slowly twisted my neck back and forth, hoping to work out the kinks, the stiffness. And when I looked up…Lord, what was wrong with that woman? She was still smiling at me. Maybe it was true what some were saying, that this wife of a mystic preacher man was a nut-job.

Ah, I'd almost forgotten about the preacher man, the spiritual leader of his flock, a pastor who liked to yell, "Fire!" just before he pushed a parishioner to the ground—his way of getting worshippers to submit to him and God. He was masterful at that, also quite adept at preaching his swindler's message of the ten-percent tithe.

The preacher man was standing beside his Tammy Faye, sporting a standoffish attitude. His dark brown eyes glanced up, then down—looking me over, I surmised, trying to take measure of my madness. There were no worry lines on his face, no tears, no fear of retribution from either man or God.

I took another deep breath, said the Lord's Prayer, and then looked toward him again. I thought it was bizarre, that I'd gone down the rabbit hole and encountered the Queen of Hearts and her hatchet and the Mad Hatter, disguised now as the preacher man. It was weird, his acting as if nothing out of the ordinary had happened. He seemed unfazed, as if the killing of another child was an everyday, common occurrence. It was as if he and the Queen were about to say, "So, why are you here? This is just a preliminary hearing for Andrew's bail." I wondered if this was what I'd have to look forward to in the months ahead. Seeming endless court appearances with these court jesters.

My head hurt. My stomach ached. I felt deathly sick.

And then our case was called. But the London's' lawyers were not present in the courtroom, so the DA motioned to reschedule.

Outside the courtroom I was told the absence of London's defense counsel could have been either a schedule conflict or unpaid retainers. So, I left, feeling emptier than before—numb, really, as I made the long walk through cold, wood-paneled chambers and well-used lobbies.

Upon my arrival home, I received a call from the DA, who told me that the London's lawyers showed up after we left, and that they motioned for Andrew's release.

For some reason, the lawyers' tardiness had a ring of dishonesty to me; it also had the appearance of being planned, not to mention calculating and inhuman.

But that was what I was dealing with—grief had to play second-fiddle to injudicious selfish concerns and courtroom antics.

43 Dreams

I enter this golden, sunlit room, and Adam is sitting on the couch, wearing shorts and no shirt. His hair is messed up—morning hair, that's how Anna used to describe it—and he stares at me, a smile on his face.

I approach, and hold him in my arms. I don't remember if we speak or not, but I do remember the hug. It is an enduring hug, seemingly without end.

And then, in a white flash of light, I awoke.

Adam is gone. I let out a deep sigh because it felt good to hold my son once again.

I am sitting in bed with Adam's lifeless body next to me, looking down at his feet. As I reach out to him, his foot moves—ever so slightly, as if he wants to tell me something.

Maybe it's just some sort of muscle contraction, the kind I've heard occur shortly after death.

As I turn my head toward Adam's face, he lifts his left arm, and his eyes snap open. And then he leans towards me.

"He's alive, alive!" I yell, hoping Anna and the girls will hear me and come running. But they don't.

So, I turn to Adam and ask, "Have you met God?"

He smiles and says, "No, Dad, but he knows who I am."

My joy is so enormous, knowing without question that Adam is happy in his heavenly home. Praying that Anna and the girls will soon arrive, so they can see what I am seeing, I continue to yell, "Adam is alive! Adam is alive!"

The door opens. It is Olivia. When she sees Adam, she is overcome with joy and runs away to get her mother and sisters.

Suddenly, I am outside our home, peering up at the most dazzling bright-blue sky I've ever seen. And there, in the middle of the sky, is a ball of intense white light. I do not know why this ball of light appears to be so exactly in the middle of the sky, it just seems important.

And it was.

You see, Olivia, is now the middle child.

I sat in the steam room asking God to bring Adam to me. I woke the next morning at four am to find that Sofia had come down and crawled into the bed. Hugging her, I fell back to sleep.

I hear myself telling the kids, "It's time to go, come on." I turn around and there is Adam leading his three sisters along a terrace. I begin descending a set of junk stairs. They are rickety, broken, creaking like old cart wheels, they are about to give way. The children must see the danger. I reach the foot of the staircase, turn to warn them, shouting, "Be careful." A transformation has occurred, and the stairway is now a mix of perfection, gold and blue Spanish tiles clad the risers, now ascending to a marble room. A brilliant glow comes from behind the children as they walk along. Adam is standing at the top. He spreads out his bare arms, forming a human cross: the light is so brilliant, his body has become a silhouette. He stands there for awhile as the radiance bleeds over him. He then descends slowly; when he reaches the bottom, he has two wooden fishing poles. He hands me one. We both turn to find a sparkling, aqua-blue lake, the sun reflecting within its surface. Adam pulls back the pole, casting the line out deep. As his hook drops in, the water ripples, one circle after another, their penumbras never fading. We fall back on some kind of bench; I am next to him, I feel his warmth. I look into his lilt face. He smiles, and then he says in his just-the-other-day voice, "Do you love the Dukee?" I lean close. Taste his breath and kiss him on his rosy cheek, and then he is gone.

I awoke, opened my eyes and I thanked God for bringing Adam to me. I shook Anna to wake her, telling her Adam was ok, and how we were fishing.

I have been praying for more visions ever since the first one in May; praying to see Adam once again, if only in my sleep. Maybe this is God's way of giving me peace; I believe it is. I record each experience, doing so with such loving care that tears are running down my face as the sun rises on the word.

44 Adam's Love Letter

August 18, 2009

I found one of Adam's letters on his computer, a message of love to his darling Stephanie. This letter touched me deeply.

Dear love of my life,

Stephanie, I love you. You have no idea how it feels to say those words to you. When I say those words, it's not just a phrase; when I say those words to you, I feel like I am conducting an orchestra, the orchestra to our happiness. Time stands still and I think of every emotion that I have had, and nothing compares to that lyric that I sing to you. I feel an overwhelming amount of joy and happiness rushing through me.

Stephanie, you are truly the most beautiful girl in the world and definitely without a doubt the cutest girl ever. Who knew that I would find the love of my life at my best friend's house? From that night on, I couldn't stop thinking and talking about the delicate Venus that you are. I have found my true love, my Stephy, my beautiful bride-to-be.

When I gaze into your amber-colored eyes, I feel like I am in space, like I have the ability to peer into your soul as if we are connected through some mystical bond.

Stephanie, I love that name. That's the name I chant when I wake up. When I say your beautiful name, this huge smile emerges on my face. Stephanie is the last word, the last phrase, I murmur when I fall asleep.

When I stand or lie down next to you, I feel so good inside. When I am next to you, I can talk about anything; my heart just pumps out words. I love our heart-to-heart conversations when we're together. They make me fall even more in love with you.

I can't wait to share every emotion with you. You're perfect in every way.

I can't wait to marry you. It will be the happiest day of our lives. I will propose to you in front of thousands of people on a stage with your favorite band behind me. I will stick with you through the good times and the hard times, but I know that we, so strong in love, can accomplish anything.

I will hold your hand forever, and I will never let go. I will always be there for you. You can always trust me. I LOVE YOU, Stephanie Goins.

LOVE,
Adam D. Stephens

45 Return to the Water

June 23, 2009

This was our first family outing since Adam's passing. Leaving home without him didn't seem right but also was necessary—without seeing him with pillow and iPod in hand, and taking his usual seat behind Anna.

Olivia sensed this also. She stared at Adam's empty seat, so unsure of herself, and then timidly asked, "Should I sit here?"

The drive was quiet, its stillness filled with memories of our family's loss. Along the way, Anna just stared out the window, tears and her whimpers breaking the uncomfortable stillness.

Olivia, understanding her mother's pain, extended her legs between the two of us. I held her feet, as if they were the very essence of life.

We arrived at St. Simons, Georgia in the dim light of early evening—only five of us now. We were by ourselves, without the intrusive and watchful eyes of others. We looked at one another, relieved to not be surrounded by sympathetic well-wishers or at our ever-remindful home.

For some time, Anna had yearned for the solitude and endless horizons of the ocean. Once she took a quick look inside the beach house, she and Sofia went straight to the beach. I allowed them their solitude and remained at the house with Hanna and Olivia, imagining the healing quality that Anna and Sofia were experiencing. I could hear the sounds that only oceans and wind can provide: the surge of surf brushing against the sandy shoreline, before retreating to a peaceful ocean.

The next day we slept till noon. I had not slept that long in years. In truth, I had slept little in the past month. Finally, walking to the beach at low tide, we just stood there mesmerized by the sand and sky and sea, each of us lost in our own thoughts.

Adam was on my mind, as I was sure he was on all our minds. It didn't seem right that we should lose him after only eighteen years. I remembered all of the joys we shared at this very spot, such a short time ago. It was as if he was standing there with me right then. I could see his face, his smiling eyes with their unbounded joy, morning hair, standing there in his bathing suit, bare-chested. I imagined him sorting out the timbers, rope and stakes, performing our ritual of setting up the homemade sun-shade—father and son, doing all we could to make the ladies in our life comfortable. Our last act was raising his special flag, the Jolly Roger.

I wish I could embrace him once again. The memories of his parting washed over me.

In front of us, a tidal current flowed from the marshlands tributary. Uprooted reeds surged past, rushing to the distant sea. Across the tidal stream, a sandbar raised up, a place of solitude from which white-crested ocean waves broke up on a distant shore. We judged the swim from where we were to there. It seemed somewhat impossible, yet absolutely necessary, for us to make the crossing.

Standing in the waist-deep water, Olivia shouted, "We can make it!"

So I started swimming; Olivia was soon at my side, matching me stroke for stroke—in tandem, father and daughter indelibly linked. And then, Anna and Sofia were braving the current, yet Hanna refused to let go of her safe domain. She waited and watched, contemplating the danger in silence.

As soon as my toes brushed the safety of the opposite

shore, my immediate concern was for Olivia. There she was, gleefully swimming toward me. With arms stretched, our fingers grasped each other. Her smile said it all—she knew I'd always be there for her.

I glanced toward shore, hoping Hanna was about to join us. But she was walking away, our distance becoming greater and greater.

Anna and Sofia had almost reached the sandbar, battling against the tidal current. As Olivia and I walked slowly to the other side of the sandbar, a soft wind blew coolly against our backs.

Anna and Olivia soon entered ocean waters, but Sofia wanted no part of it. It was as if she was saying, "Once was enough, Dad." She stood fast at the ocean's edge, the waves breaking against her shins.

"Come on in, it's okay," I pled with her, hoping she'd join me. But some fear seemed to get the better of her. Her wide-eyed look told me she needed me—without fail, right then. So I walked to her, in the shallowest of waters, and we sat together, side-by-side, in the wet sand.

"Can I cover you with sand?" I asked.

She didn't answer. Instead, she laid down and let the surf brush over her, just enough to stay cool and wet.

The fine-grain sand was almost like mud, and I scooped up a handful and put it on her belly, then her legs and arms, rubbing it in to soothe her sunned skin. Gradually, her fear subsided; she relaxed, was relieved. And time passed just like that.

When I looked back across to the opposite shore, Hanna was gliding toward us—her sixteen-year-old figure had made headway against the surf, cutting through the current with strong, measured strokes, triumphantly overcoming whatever misgivings she'd wrestled with.

And when she finally joined us, I was struck with the realization that we were, once again, a family, together on this island in a troubled sea. Most certainly not as whole as we once were, but we were gradually moving forward despite the loss of one integral part.

Hanna was next to be buried by sand. And although she at first complained about the mud getting on her bathing suit, she soon acted as if it was no big deal. Again, I was struck by the realization that all Hanna really cared about at that moment was my attention.

Olivia, who had been watching while frolicking in the deeper surf, finally joined us. Much to her delight, Hanna and Sofia and I took turns covering her with sand. And when she asked me to rub her feet, I complied—ever so gently.

Such was the beginning of our passage, with Adam looking down on us.

As Anna sat in the surf, alone with her own thoughts, little Sofia suddenly got up and ran to her. All she needed was a hug from her Mama.

46 Adam's Birthday

Today is September 23, 2009, Adam's birthday.

On this day, nineteen years ago, Anna and I were blessed with one of the sweetest dreams-come-true that any couple could ever be blessed with. And on this special day, we always woke him while holding lit candles, smiling as he rose, and singing "Happy Birthday."

Giving him a moment alone, we would gather upstairs around the dining room table, awaiting his entrance. It was a family ritual. He would join us in his underwear, take a seat at the end of the table and then, without hesitation, put on this silly birthday hat—hats that Anna made sure everyone wore, silly sort of honor.

His gifts were set out under multi-colored birthday lights and on a sea of his favorite candy. He opened his presents, then got ready for school. I would come home early from work to pick him up and take him and the family wherever he wanted to go for dinner. And afterwards, we went home to the cake that Anna had made.

And then, once again, we would sing "Happy Birthday."

It was a ritual—just one of many childish, yet enjoyable family ceremonies we relished in the Stephens household.

Today, however, I awake and walk into Adam's room, my fingers lightly brushing the things I know he touched often. But as I put on one of his shirts to wear in honor of his birth, I break down and cry.

You would think I'd have run out of tears by now. But no.

I relive the moment of Adam's birth, experience, once again, the thrill of seeing him first stand on his own, and then, later, eventually take his first steps on wobbly legs.

I see him riding across the grass on his bicycle, his smile

never ceasing as he rode off. Of course, I trailed behind him, just to make sure he did not fall. And I see his broken-hearted reaction, his tears at the end of the play Of Mice and Men, when Lenny gets shot.

I remember his joy in helping me set up the beach shade, and my thoughts race through the yesterdays when we sat down to dinner, just him and me, talking about nothing in particular—yet enjoying every word, every gesture.

There, proudly hanging on the wall, are his tennis rackets. As my fingers reach out, brushing against the strings, I experience once again our games together; the many courts—some near to home, others quite distant. And I reminisce about our vacations and our seemingly endless conversations—my just being there as an understanding father to such a fine, well-mannered and intelligent young boy, who rapidly became the young man expressing his love to his Stephanie.

That was my Adam, who will forever be eighteen. He was so much, but had such little time.

He is the tear I can never wipe away.

CPSIA information can be obtained at www.ICGtesting.com
Printed in the USA
LVOW05s1237190813

348493LV00004B/8/P